CAN YOU MAKE THAT GLUTEN-FREE?

MEGAN McKENNA
CAN YOU MAKE THAT GLUTEN-FREE?

80 GLUTEN-FREE RECIPES

hamlyn

First published in Great Britain in 2022 by Hamlyn,
an imprint of
Octopus Publishing Group Ltd
Carmelite House
50 Victoria Embankment
London EC4Y 0DZ
www.octopusbooks.co.uk

An Hachette UK Company
www.hachette.co.uk
www.octopusbooksusa.com

Distributed in the US by
Hachette Book Group
1290 Avenue of the Americas
4th and 5th Floors
New York, NY 10104

Distributed in Canada by
Canadian Manda Group
664 Annette St.
Toronto, Ontario, Canada M6S 2C8

ISBN 978-0-60063-738-7 (UK)
ISBN 978-0-60063-746-2 (US)

A CIP catalogue record for this book is available
from the British Library.

Printed and bound in China
10 9 8 7 6 5 4 3 2 1

Publishing Director Eleanor Maxfield
Deputy Art Director Jaz Bahra
Senior Editor Alex Stetter
Photography Louise Hagger
Props Stylist Alexander Breeze
Home Economist Becks Wilkinson
Production Manager Lisa Pinnell

Publisher's notes
Both imperial and metric measurements
have been given in all recipes. Use one set of
measurements only and not a mixture of both.

Standard level spoon measurements are used
in all recipes.

1 tablespoon = one 15 ml spoon

1 teaspoon = one 5 ml spoon

Eggs should be medium unless otherwise stated.

CONTENTS

INTRODUCTION

Hey guys, as you may be aware, I can't eat gluten or wheat, and yes, it can make me (and anyone else with this problem) a little cranky when offered a lettuce leaf as an alternative to standard dishes. So it feels amazing to finally be writing this gluten-free cookbook; it's something I've wanted to do for ages! Years of showing people my cooking videos on social media and loads of messages asking 'Can you make that gluten-free?' have led to this moment, and I can now share all my secrets with you.

I'm not pointing the finger at anyone here, but a lot of people get scared and only want to offer us GF peeps something plain or dry that could pass as animal food. Well, times have changed and I'm here to help. There's no longer any need to feel left out on pancake day. And you can forget those years when you had to go without a birthday cake, or were unable to eat the food at parties and other events. Now you can tuck into breaded chicken or gooey mac & cheese with none of the worry,

because I have GF recipes for those things and loads of other mouth-watering food.

I'll never be able to erase the memory of sitting all alone in the stairwell at secondary school, eating my packed lunch of chicken or veg because the canteen couldn't cater for me and I didn't want to stand out from the other kids. I wanted to eat 'normal' food and not have people ask 'What's that in your lunchbox?' You see, back then GF bread was awful; it was rock hard and tasted like stale cake. It's so much better now! I was already having a hard time at school without being a 'GF freak' too, so I kept myself to myself and quickly scoffed my food away from others. Sometimes, though, I didn't eat at all, which would give me migraines. What a nightmare!

I was always a happy child, growing up in the countryside with my mum and grandparents. Granddad grew his own vegetables and cooked amazing curries, while Mum and Nanny baked fantastic cakes, biscuits and puddings.

Flavoursome food was a constant in our family, but I spent years being unwell, going through numerous tests at the hospital, where they thought I had Crohn's disease. It turned out I had a wheat allergy and was coeliac (unable to process gluten). I won't go into detail, but let's just say the bathroom was my best friend when I was growing up. Even now, I have my ups and downs. After I was given the correct diagnosis, my mum taught me how to cook everything from scratch, and this is why I'm so confident at cooking. My talented sister Milly, who is a cook too, has also been teaching me various tricks in the kitchen for a while now. Our mum taught us well!

Since stepping into the limelight via reality TV, I've had more than my fair share of trolling, tantrums and toilets. For a long time I've been called skeletal, anorexic and gaunt. Hmm, maybe people need to lay off the weight comments and give those who suffer silently with digestive issues a break. It's taken me years to get to a healthy position, and that's why I wanted to do this book so much. I've been following a strict gluten-free and wheat-free diet for years and discovered that if you swap a few ingredients here and there in standard recipes, you can make *anything* GF! In fact, I highly recommend you purchase a few extra copies and post them to your nearest and dearest so they have no excuses for not producing suitable food when you go over to eat, hahaha! Anyway, enough about me.

Welcome to my kitchen – and let's start cooking things that can change your life!

Megan x

MY TOP 10 TIPS

Over the years, I've learnt a few things about being gluten-free. I love going out to eat, but it can be quite tricky, especially if people in restaurants don't understand what gluten can actually do to some of us! Being a coeliac, eating gluten can cause all sorts of issues and we don't want any mistakes.

HERE ARE MY TOP TIPS:

1   Even when menus state that chips are GF, always check which oil they're being fried in. The cook may be using the same oil in which they fry food that isn't gluten-free, and this can end up pretty messy.

2   Ring restaurants before you go to pre-warn them, so they can cater for you as well as possible.

3   Some gluten-free loafs aren't the softest, so zap your bread for a few minutes in the microwave. It gets so soft, you might mistake it for the real thing, haha.

4   Check people's toasters! If you're at a café, ask them to either use a

toastie bag or a different toaster for your brekkie. If that's not possible, buttered GF bread it is.

5   Become an avid reader of labels. You'd be surprised what has gluten and wheat in it– even some chewy sweets and beauty products do! Being a coeliac means you also can't eat other grains like barley and so on, so make sure you check up on that if you have been diagnosed.

6   A lot of vodkas contain wheat and gluten – even the cute shots like Tequila Rose. So when it comes to alcohol, read the label and be careful what you're putting in your mouth.

7   When you're making gluten-free pasta, add a few drops of olive oil to the cooking water – gluten-free pasta can become clumpy, and the oil stops the pasta from sticking together.

8   I always zap my gluten-free cookies in the microwave for a few minutes before I eat them, to make them hot and soft again!

9   Always carry Buscopan and Imodium. You never know when you might have an emergency. This is aimed at the IBS crew – I feel you.

10   Remember, lots of foods are naturally GF, such as veg and meat, but check processed meats, as even sausages ofen have wheat in them!

Welcome to my gluten-free kitchen – now let's start cooking things that will change your life!

RECIPES

BREAKFAST CLUB

Here are my favourite breakfast recipes, and yessss, don't stress ... I have included my famous pancake and bacon recipe! I'm all for healthy eating, but I'm also in favour of maple syrup.

I never used to like breakfast food, and got to the point where I ate dinner-type things instead. Cafés certainly didn't cater well for the GF gang, and some still don't. It really isn't that hard to change a few ingredients over to make us pancakes and a club sandwich!

Creating easy morning dishes, from spicy salmon slices to avocado on toast, has made me fall in love with breakfast. It's just what I need first thing! And if your naughty side is piping up, I've got that covered too. Travelling the world has opened my eyes and my taste buds to sweetness and spice and everything nice! In Nashville I was introduced to pouring syrup all over my bacon and eggs, while in LA I was sipping celery juice with the cool kids. I've put my GF twist on all the recipes that follow so we can enjoy them together!

TABASCO SALMON SLICES

I like my spice, can you tell? I wasn't always a fan of smoked salmon on toast, but this fiery way of eating it takes it to a whole other level. It's a healthy way to start the day, and also great as a quick bite at other times!

SERVES 2

2 slices of gluten-free bread

60 g (2¼ oz) cream cheese

40 g (1½ oz) smoked salmon pieces

juice of ½ lemon

1 teaspoon gluten-free Tabasco sauce

½ teaspoon black pepper

Toast your bread.

Spread evenly with your cream cheese, then top with your salmon.

Squeeze your lemon juice over, then sprinkle the Tabasco and black pepper across both slices.

Slice into 'soldiers' or triangles and serve.

MEGAN'S FAMOUS PANCAKES

Well, here you go – my GF pancakes that I literally live on five days a week. They are so good, and fluffy too! The demand for these bad boys has been crazy. Pair them with my crispy bacon and maple syrup (opposite)!

MAKES 12

450 g (1 lb) gluten-free self-raising flour

2 eggs

300 ml (10 fl oz) semi-skimmed milk

olive oil, for frying

Put your flour, eggs and milk into a large bowl and whisk until smooth.

Place 1 tablespoon olive oil in a large non-stick pan over a low heat. When hot, add 1 heaped tablespoon of your pancake batter and swirl it into a small circle about 5 mm (¼ in) thick. Depending on the size of the pan, add another 1 or 2 spoonfuls in the same way. The circles look thin, but they will rise, don't you worry!

Turn the heat up to medium and cook for about 1½ minutes on each side, until fluffed up and lightly speckled brown. You'll know when they're ready.

Transfer the pancakes to a plate and keep warm while you make as many more pancakes as you can with the remaining batter. Remember to heat a spoonful of oil for each batch.

Serve the pancakes with your chosen toppings (*see* opposite and pages 24–5).

AMERICAN CRISPY BACON & SYRUP

You won't ever eat boring bacon again once you've tried this style. Salty but smoked, this bacon melts in your mouth, and don't forget to add maple syrup – a true American twist! This is my go-to topping for pancakes.

SERVES 2–4 AS A SIDE ————————————————————————

1 tablespoon olive oil

1 x 200 g (7 oz) pack streaky smoked bacon

maple syrup, for drizzling

strawberries, for garnish (optional)

Heat your olive oil in a frying pan over a medium heat. When hot, add your bacon and cook for 6–7 minutes, turning as needed.

Once golden and crisp, drain on kitchen paper, then serve on top of your fluffy pancakes with a drizzle of maple syrup.

If you want to be extra fancy, cut up some strawberries and add them too.

FIRE AVOCADO

I like to add a kick to my food here and there, and avocado was a good place to start as I really didn't like it before I tried it this way. Mixing it with the right ingredients will make it light up your mouth! Serve on toast or pancakes, or with tortilla chips as a snack, or even as a side dish.

SERVES 2 AS A SIDE

1 large or 2 small avocados, halved and stoned

½ red onion, finely diced

5 cherry tomatoes, chopped

juice of ½ lemon

1 tablespoon gluten-free Tabasco sauce

2 pinches sea salt flakes

1 teaspoon black pepper

Using a tablespoon, scoop the avocado flesh into a bowl, then use the side of the spoon to roughly chop it. You want it to be chunky, not mashed.

Add the red onion and tomatoes, followed by the lemon juice and Tabasco.

Season with the salt and pepper and mix well, keeping the avocado nice and chunky.

ROASTED VINE TOMATOES

Some mornings, this style of breakfast is a fave. Pairing these tomatoes and the mushrooms below with my Fire Avocado mix (opposite) makes for a light but filling healthy start to the day. Serve on toast or pancakes, or as a side dish.

SERVES 2 AS A SIDE

2 stems of baby tomatoes on the vine

1 teaspoon olive oil

1 teaspoon sea salt flakes

Preheat your oven to 180°C/160°C Fan (350°F), Gas Mark 4.

Place your tomatoes, still on the vine, in a roasting tray, drizzle the oil over them and sprinkle with your salt.

Roast for 15–20 minutes, until your tomatoes are just splitting and look golden on top.

BALSAMIC MUSHROOMS

It's all in the seasoning – you can make simple ingredients into gourmet meals in minutes. Another beautiful side dish to go with any meal!

SERVES 2 AS A SIDE

4 large mushrooms, peeled

gluten-free balsamic glaze

garlic granules

sea salt flakes and pepper

Preheat your oven to 180°C/160°C Fan (350°F), Gas Mark 4.

Place the mushrooms in a roasting tray, gill-side up, and drizzle generously with balsamic glaze.

Lightly sprinkle with your garlic granules and season well.

Roast for 20 minutes until softened and juicy.

CELERY JUICE

You'll need a juicer for this one, but it's a great investment, as celery juice is pure goodness in a glass and has been proven to help all sorts of problems! Apart from being packed with vitamins and boosting your immune system, it helps to balance blood sugar levels and protect against type 2 diabetes and heart disease. I drink this a few times a week before I eat anything. It's the most effective way to get all that goodness!

SERVES 1–2

1 whole head of celery

½ cup ice

juice of ½ lime

Cut off the base of the celery, then cut off and discard the leafy bits. Wash the stalks and cut them into thirds.

Put a few pieces into your juicer and whizz to create a liquid.

Fill a glass with the ice, pour in your celery juice, stir in your lime juice and drink immediately.

TENNESSEE BEANS ON TOAST

Who wants boring beans? Adding a few additional ingredients will make your breakfast more gourmet! Posh beans on toast, anyone?

SERVES 2

1 x 415 g (14½ oz) can baked beans

2 teaspoons gluten-free barbecue sauce

1 teaspoon chilli flakes

2 slices of gluten-free bread

butter, for spreading (optional)

50 g (2 oz) Cheddar cheese

sea salt flakes and pepper

Place your beans in a saucepan and add your barbecue sauce and chilli flakes. Stir over a low-medium heat for 8–10 minutes, until your beans develop a thicker consistency.

Toast your bread and butter it, if you like, then place on 2 plates and top with the beans.

Grate the cheese over, then add a pinch of salt and a crack of black pepper.

BREAKFAST CLUB SANDWICH

Here is my take on a club sandwich, the one sandwich I always look for when I'm out, and that cafés never seem to get quite right. Stack it up and take a huge bite!

SERVES 1–2

3 tablespoons olive oil

3 slices of smoked bacon

1 egg

3 slices of gluten-free bread

butter, for spreading

1 tablespoon gluten-free mayonnaise

1 teaspoon gluten-free ketchup

2 lettuce leaves

2 slices of tomato

2 slices of cheese

salt and pepper

Heat 2 tablespoons of your olive oil in a frying pan and fry your bacon over a medium heat for 6–7 minutes, turning once. Transfer to a plate and keep warm.

Heat the remaining oil in the frying pan and fry your egg over a medium heat for 4 minutes, until the white is set. Flip it over and fry for a further 4 minutes. You want the yolk just a tad moist, not runny! Season with salt and pepper.

Meanwhile, toast your bread and spread the slices with butter and then mayonnaise. Spread just 1 slice with your ketchup.

Place the ketchup slice on a plate and add 1 lettuce leaf, half the tomato slices, bacon and cheese. Repeat with the second slice, the remaining lettuce, tomato, bacon and cheese and then top with your egg!

Finally, cover with the remaining slice of toast. Cut in half and enjoy!

LEMON & SUGAR PANCAKES

I'm all for chocolate on thin pancakes, but this way of enjoying them is sweet and sour, which I think is the best way to eat them. Make sure you are generous with the lemon and sugar! These are a true fave!

MAKES 6–8 CRÊPES

200 g (7 oz) gluten-free flour

2 eggs

200 ml (7 fl oz) milk

4½ tablespoons water

olive oil, for frying

1 lemon, cut into wedges

4 tablespoons white caster sugar

Place your flour in a large bowl, add your eggs, milk and water and whisk until you have a smooth batter.

Heat ½ teaspoon olive oil in a frying pan over a medium-high heat.

Add 1 ladleful of batter to the middle of your pan and tilt it around to make a large circle going right to the edge.

Cook for about 1 minute on each side, until lightly golden.

Transfer to a plate and keep warm while you make the remaining pancakes in the same way.

Serve with a squeeze of lemon juice and a sprinkling of sugar. Alternatively, serve with chocolate and hazelnut spread if you fancy a chocolate hit!

HOT CHOCOLATE WITH CREAM & MARSHMALLOWS

This is the best hot chocolate ever!

SERVES 1

3 heaped teaspoons hot chocolate powder

150 ml (5 fl oz) milk of your choice (I love using soy milk for this)

50 ml (2 fl oz) boiling water

ready-whipped cream or vegan alternative

1 handful mini marshmallows

Place your chocolate powder in your favourite cup. (This drink looks cute in a tall coffee glass, if you have one.)

Heat your milk in a small saucepan until almost boiling. Take off the heat and froth using a mini electric whisk or the frother on a coffee machine.

Add your boiling water to the cup and stir to dissolve the chocolate power, then top up with your frothy milk.

Squirt some whipped cream on top, add your marshmallows and drink up!

RECIVES

QUICK BITES

Do you ever come in from work and have no energy to stand at the cooker? Well, I've sorted your problem. This section is full of dishes that are easy, quick to make and very, very tasty – from a coconut curry to sausage pasta, and even a warming winter soup that is so easy, I could make it with my eyes closed. I obviously wouldn't advise that, but you get what I mean.

Just because you feel lazy, doesn't mean you have to eat lazy. No microwaved dishes allowed here! Processed food isn't good for us GF people, or anyone else for that matter. Another thing with my recipes is that you don't have to worry about being satisfied, as (thanks to my mum) the quantities are on the generous side, and you can always save leftovers for lunch the next day. My vegetable soup, for example, makes enough for a whole weekend and can be stored in the fridge, or frozen for future use. Never waste food! Apart from the salads, everything in this chapter stores brilliantly in the freezer.

As ever, you'll find a world of flavour in the following recipes, and I've included a number of my favourites, especially saucy dishes that I feel it's hard to get GF versions of when eating out. Be adventurous and enjoy!

VEG SOUP TO LAST A WEEKEND

You can't beat a homemade vegetable soup. It's full of goodness, makes you feel warm to the core and is great for staying trim. I even cook this up in the summer – it's so quick and easy to heat up for a light lunch!

SERVES 4

3 tablespoons olive oil

2 garlic cloves, finely chopped

1 fresh chilli, finely chopped

1 large onion, roughly chopped

4 carrots, peeled and thickly sliced

4 celery sticks, thickly sliced

5 parsnips, thickly sliced

50 ml (2 fl oz) gluten-free soy sauce

50 ml (2 fl oz) gluten-free Worcestershire sauce

1 litre (35 fl oz) gluten-free chicken stock

½ head of sweetheart cabbage, finely sliced

1 tablespoon honey

1 heaped tablespoon chilli flakes

salt and pepper

Place your oil in a large saucepan over a medium heat. When the oil is hot, add the garlic and chopped chilli to the pan and fry for 2 minutes.

Add your onion and fry for another few minutes until translucent.

Add your carrots, celery and parsnips and fry for 2–3 minutes.

Now add your soy sauce and Worcestershire sauce and season well with pepper.

Pour in your stock, then add your cabbage and stir well.

Add your honey and chilli flakes, and generously season again with black pepper and a big pinch of salt.

Bring to the boil, then simmer for 1½ hours. Serve straight away, or leave to cool, then refrigerate and reheat as needed.

BUTTERNUT SQUASH COCONUT CURRY

Oh, wow – how I love this dish! It's so easy to make, full of goodness and so tasty! It's a winner!

SERVES 2

1 x 600 g (1 lb 5 oz) butternut squash

5 cm (2 in) piece fresh ginger, peeled and finely chopped

2 garlic cloves, finely chopped

½ tablespoon ground turmeric

½ tablespoon dried coriander

olive oil, for frying

1 teaspoon sugar

2 teaspoons garam masala

3 teaspoons curry powder

1 onion, diced

1 hot chilli, finely diced

1 x 400 g (14 oz) can chickpeas

1 x 400 ml (14 fl oz) can coconut milk

15 g (½ oz) fresh coriander, chopped, plus extra for garnish

2 tablespoons gluten-free soy sauce

100 ml (3½ fl oz) hot gluten-free chicken or vegetable stock

1 lime

Preheat your oven to 180°C/160°C Fan (350°F), Gas Mark 4.

Halve and seed the squash (there's no need to peel it), then cut into bite-sized chunks and lay out on a baking tray. Season well with pepper and place in the oven for 45 minutes.

Place the ginger, garlic, turmeric and dried coriander in a large pan with a generous splash of olive oil and cook for about 1 minute.

Add the sugar, garam masala and curry powder, and allow them to cook out and infuse the mixture for 2–3 minutes.

Add the onion and chilli, plus more oil if needed, and fry for 5 minutes.

Drain the chickpeas and tip them into the pan along with your coconut milk, chopped coriander, soy sauce and stock. Leave to simmer over a low heat for 15 minutes.

Once your butternut squash is done, add it to the curry and cook for a further 5 minutes.

Squeeze in the juice of half a lime. Taste the sauce and, if necessary, add some salt. Slice the remaining lime and use it to garnish before serving, along with extra coriander.

GOATS' CHEESE, BEETROOT & CARAMELIZED WALNUT SALAD

Even though this is an easy recipe, it looks very impressive, especially with the caramelized nuts! It's the perfect fancy salad to serve if you have friends coming over. Go you!

SERVES 1–2

120 g (4¼ oz) white caster sugar

120 g (4¼ oz) shelled walnuts

1 tablespoon water

100 g (3½ oz) goats' cheese

5 Baby Gem lettuce leaves

3 pre-cooked baby beetroot

2 tablespoons gluten-free balsamic glaze

Preheat your oven to 180°C/160°C Fan (350°F), Gas Mark 4.

Place your sugar, walnuts and water in a pan over a medium heat and stir until the sugar has dissolved and no grains remain.

Make sure every walnut is coated in the sugar syrup, then transfer to a baking sheet and roast for 10 minutes.

Allow the nuts to cool a little, then coarsely crush them with a rolling pin and set aside.

Place your goats' cheese in a baking dish in the oven for 5 minutes.

Meanwhile, place your lettuce leaves on a serving plate, overlapping them for a rustic look, if you like.

When your cheese has cooked for 5 minutes, add your beets and warm through, about 3 more minutes.

Place your cheese in the middle of your lettuce. Roughly chop the beets and sprinkle them around it.

Drizzle your glaze over the whole dish and sprinkle with your crushed walnuts. Yummy!

COURGETTI BOLOGNESE

Spag bol who? This is the new way to eat bolognese and is *far* healthier than the usual pasta-based recipe. I eat this at least once a week; it's become a family fave. I pair it with my Rocket & Balsamic Salad (*see* opposite) – they taste great together!

SERVES 4

olive oil, for frying

400 g (14 oz) minced beef (12% fat)

1 x 500g (1 lb 2 oz) jar gluten-free tomato pasta sauce

4 courgettes

300 ml (10 fl oz) semi-skimmed milk

1 heaped tablespoon cornflour

40 g (1½ oz) Cheddar cheese

salt and pepper

Preheat your oven to 180°C/160°C Fan (350°F), Gas Mark 4.

Place 2 tablespoons olive oil in a saucepan over a medium heat. When hot, add your minced beef and season with 2 pinches of salt and a generous crack of black pepper. Stir and break up your mince as it cooks and browns.

Add the tomato sauce, stir until it bubbles, then simmer for 10 minutes over a low heat.

Meanwhile, slice your courgettes in half lengthways and lay them in a baking tray, cut side up. Place in the oven for 15 minutes.

While the sauce and courgettes are cooking, pour your milk into a saucepan, add the cornflour and whisk well. Season well with pepper, then place over a medium heat and keep stirring until you notice the mixture has thickened and coats the back of a spoon.

Remove the tray of courgettes from the oven. Using a spoon, scoop out the middle of the courgettes and stir into the sauce.

Fill your courgettes with your bolognese sauce, then dollop a spoonful of your white sauce on each one and grate over some of the Cheddar. Finish with a crack of black pepper and pop the courgettes back in the oven for 30–35 minutes, until they're golden brown on top.

ROCKET & BALSAMIC SALAD

This is the perfect side dish to accompany a light lunch or tasty pasta. The peppery flavour of the rocket works brilliantly with the sweetness of the balsamic!

SERVES 2–4 AS A SIDE

1 x 60 g (2¼ oz) bag rocket

extra virgin olive oil

gluten-free balsamic glaze

sea salt flakes and black pepper

Place your rocket on a medium plate or in a bowl.

Add olive oil and balsamic glaze to your liking. I tend to pour a light drizzle of oil across the whole salad, then squeeze my balsamic glaze back and forth so it covers the majority of the leaves.

Crack black pepper across your salad and add a big pinch of sea salt flakes.

MOZZARELLA & TOMATO SALAD

You can't beat a true Italian salad – simple but full of flavour and it looks so pretty on the plate, too. I always feel the freshness of the tomatoes and creaminess of the cheese complements any pasta or chicken dish. Adding the pesto gives this an extra special touch.

SERVES 2

2 beef tomatoes, sliced 1 cm (½ in) thick

1 x 125 g (4½ oz) ball mozzarella cheese, drained and sliced 1 cm (½ in) thick

2 tablespoons gluten-free basil pesto

2 tablespoons extra virgin olive oil

handful of fresh basil leaves

sea salt flakes and pepper

Arrange your tomatoes on a serving plate. Break your mozzarella slices into pieces and dot them evenly across the tomatoes.

Using a teaspoon, place a tiny blob of pesto on every other piece of mozzarella.

Drizzle your olive oil across the whole salad.

Sprinkle over your basil leaves and finish with a big pinch of salt and a generous crack of black pepper.

STIR-FRY SOUP BOWL

There's something about the flavours and crunch of the veg in this soup that I really love. The whole thing is an explosion in your mouth, and great for a quick, easy lunch or dinner!

SERVES 2

olive oil, for frying

1 garlic clove, chopped

2.5 cm (1 in) piece fresh ginger, peeled and chopped

1 x 400 g (14 oz) bag stir-fry vegetables with beansprouts

1–2 tablespoons gluten-free soy sauce, to taste

2 x 175 g (6 oz) chicken breast fillets, cut into bite-sized pieces

2 tablespoons gluten-free sriracha

1½ tablespoons gluten-free sweet chilli sauce

1½ tablespoons gluten-free teriyaki sauce

200 ml (7 fl oz) water

Put a large frying pan over a medium heat and add a splash of olive oil. When hot, add your garlic and ginger to the pan and cook for 1–2 minutes.

Now add your bag of stir-fry mix, followed by your soy sauce. Cook for 3–4 minutes, stirring constantly, until the veg start to soften. Remove the veg from the pan and set aside.

Add the chicken to the pan with the sriracha and the sweet chilli sauce. Cook, stirring regularly, until the chicken is starting to brown and is almost cooked through.

Add the stir-fried veg back to the pan, along with the teriyaki sauce and measured water. Stir well and leave to simmer for 6–7 minutes, making sure the chicken is completely cooked through before serving.

SPICY CHORIZO & SAUSAGE PASTA

You can't go wrong with a great pasta dish, and this one is so full of flavour that you don't need anything else with it! The chorizo really carries this dish.

SERVES 2-3

olive oil, for frying

6 gluten-free caramelized onion sausages

200 g (7 oz) gluten-free penne

3 garlic cloves, finely chopped

100 g (3½ oz) cooking chorizo, chopped

1 x 400 g (14 oz) can chopped tomatoes

1 tablespoon dried mixed herbs

2 teaspoons brown sugar

1 tablespoon tomato purée

2 teaspoons chilli flakes

20 g (¾ oz) fresh basil, roughly chopped or torn, plus extra to garnish

200 ml (7 fl oz) double cream

salt and pepper

Parmesan cheese, to serve

Heat a splash of olive oil in a frying pan. When hot, add your sausages and cook for about 12 minutes, turning frequently, until nicely browned and cooked through. Set aside on a plate.

Bring a large pan of water to the boil, salt generously, then add your pasta and cook until al dente. All gluten-free pastas cook differently; I cook mine for just under 10 minutes, but check yours after 6 minutes, and keep checking every minute until the texture is soft but still with some bite. You don't want it so soft that it breaks.

Place a splash of olive oil in a large, clean frying pan and fry your garlic and chorizo for 2–3 minutes.

Add your tomatoes, dried mixed herbs, brown sugar, tomato purée and chilli flakes and mix well.

Stir in your basil and leave the sauce to simmer for another 2–3 minutes.

Slice your cooked sausages and add them to your sauce.

Stir in your cream and leave to simmer for 2 more minutes.

Strain your pasta, add to your sauce and stir well.

Season generously with pepper and a pinch of salt, then add some grated Parmesan and a few basil leaves. Bon appétit!

CHILLI & SOY SALMON

Here's another easy dish that takes less than half an hour to prepare and cook. This salmon recipe is a big success in my home and it tastes great with my Spicy Noodles (*see* opposite).

SERVES 2

2 teaspoons gluten-free soy sauce

2 teaspoons gluten-free sweet chilli sauce

1 teaspoon gluten-free sriracha

2.5 cm (1 in) piece fresh ginger, peeled and finely chopped

1 teaspoon chilli flakes

2 tablespoons honey

2 x 120 g (4¼ oz) salmon fillets

Preheat your oven to 180°C/160°C Fan (350°F), Gas Mark 4. Cut 2 pieces of foil large enough to wrap around a salmon fillet.

Place your 3 sauces in a wide, shallow bowl and add your ginger, chilli flakes and honey. Mix well.

Dip your salmon into the sauce, coating both sides, and leave to soak in it for a minute.

Place each fillet, skin-side up, on a piece of foil. Raise the foil slightly around the fish, then pour the remaining sauce over them.

Seal the foil around them and bake for 20–25 minutes.

Serve the fish skin-side down, perhaps with my Rice Noodles and Garlic-Sautéd Green Beans (see opposite and page 114).

SPICY NOODLES

I don't know about you, but I find it pretty difficult to get gluten-free noodles when I'm out and about. Maybe one day restaurants will get better at catering for us GF people, but when I'm at home, I love to cook these to get my noodle fix. Sometimes, I even eat them with chopsticks to make the whole experience more real, haha!

SERVES 2

1 tablespoon olive oil

1 garlic clove, chopped

2.5 cm (1 in) piece fresh ginger, peeled and chopped

1 x 300 g (10½ oz) bag stir-fry vegetables with beansprouts

1 red chilli, chopped

4 teaspoons gluten-free soy sauce

4 teaspoons gluten-free sweet chilli sauce

1 tablespoon gluten-free sriracha

3 tablespoons honey

150 g (5¼ oz) soft, ready to stir-fry rice noodles (check they're gluten-free)

1 lime, quartered

20g (¾ oz) fresh coriander, roughly chopped, plus 2 sprigs to garnish

Place a large pan over a medium heat and warm your olive oil.

When hot, add your garlic and ginger and fry for 1–2 minutes.

Add your bag of stir-fry veg, your chopped chilli and soy sauce. Stir and cook for 3–4 minutes, until the vegetables are starting to soften.

Now add your sweet chilli sauce, sriracha and honey, and cook for another 3 minutes. You'll see the veg shrink down a bit more.

Add your noodles and mix well.

Squeeze in the juice from 1 quarter of your lime, add your coriander and mix again.

Serve the noodles with a wedge of lime on the side and a sprig of coriander on top.

RECIPES

LOADED NACHOS

BEER-BATTERED
GHERKINS

CHILLI CON CARNE

TEXAS CHICKEN

ENCHILADAS

PAPRIKA POTATOES

AMERICAN LETTUCE
BURGER

SOUTHERN SLAW

MAC & CHEESE

MOZZARELLA
BREADED CHICKEN
WITH PESTO PASTA

COTTAGE PIE

SIRLOIN STEAK

TRIPLE-COOKED
CHIPS

BLUE CHEESE SAUCE

ARANCINI

CHILLI DIP

FROZEN MARGARITA

PICANTE

PORN STAR MARTINI

FROZEN STRAWBERRY
DAIQUIRI

NAUGHTY
NIGHTS IN

Who doesn't love a night in with all their favourite comfort food? These days, I actually prefer eating in front of the TV to going out, haha! I bet you never thought you'd hear me say that.

Now as you know, I'm a big fan of America, and I love all the diner food you find there. The problem is that diner food is full of gluten. Why is that, when gluten and wheat are not essential in any of these dishes? It would be so easy for restaurants and takeout places to change up their ingredients and cater for us all! But don't worry, guys, chef Megan has created diner food for your living room, from lettuce burgers with my special caramelized onions, to spicy chilli and nachos. Yum! Have you ever had a GF battered pickle before? Bet you haven't! Now it's time to try out all the naughty foods that you can't normally have.

Another element to this section is COCKTAILS! That might surprise you because some alcohol contains gluten or wheat. In fact, there was a time when I didn't know that, so for years I went partying and innocently drinking alcohol that was upsetting me. So what's the key? Try changing to tequila! Don't stress if you hate it – try my four famous party drinks, especially the frozen margaritas with sugar around the rim. These recipes not only agree with my gut, but taste unreal.

Now get your friends over and EAT!

LOADED NACHOS

OK, I'm a sucker for nachos, and for crisps and dips in general. I love to make a large portion to share (I defo eat them all) and load it with all the best bits! Add my Chilli con Carne on top if you want to go to the extreme! This is literally finger-licking goodness.

SERVES 4

180 g (6¼ oz) gluten-free salted corn chips

200 g (7 oz) ready-made hot salsa

1 x 120 g (4¼ oz) jar of jalapeño chillies

100 g (3½ oz) ready-made sour cream and chive dip (check it's gluten-free)

250 g (9 oz) Cheddar cheese

Preheat your grill to very hot, or, if you prefer, you can finish the dish in a microwave.

Lay out your corn chips on a large ovenproof plate or in a baking dish.

Spoon your salsa across the chips, leaving the odd gap.

Sprinkle with jalapeños to your liking – the more the better for me!

Now dot some of the sour cream and chive dip across your corn chips too.

Grate your cheese all over so that there are no gaps.

Place the dish under your hot grill, or microwave on High for a few minutes, until the cheese has melted and is golden brown. Both results are insane!

TIP
If you want to go extra crazy, I highly recommend you to swap out the salsa for the Chilli con Carne (*see* page 70). You can thank me later...

BEER-BATTERED GHERKINS

This is a great side for a dinner party or a cheap night in! I use a deep-fat fryer to cook the gherkins, but they can be shallow-fried if you prefer.

MAKES 6

100 g (3½ oz) gluten-free plain flour

55 ml (2¼ fl oz) gluten-free beer

½ teaspoon garlic granules

½ teaspoon chilli flakes

1 teaspoon salt

1 teaspoon pepper

6 big gherkins, about 8 x 2 cm (3 x ¾ in), in sweet vinegar

vegetable oil, for frying

Place half your flour in a bowl, add the beer, garlic granules and chilli flakes and mix to a smooth paste. Pop this in the refrigerator for 30 minutes.

Place the remaining flour in a separate bowl and stir in the salt and pepper.

Lay your gherkins on kitchen paper and pat dry.

Fill a deep-fat fryer with vegetable oil and heat to 180°C (350°F). Alternatively, pour the oil into a deep saucepan, filling it no more than one-third full, and heat until a cube of bread browns in 40–45 seconds.

Dip your gherkins in the flour, ensuring they are fully coated, then shake off the excess and dip them into your chilled batter. Lower straight into your hot oil one at a time, carefully swishing them from side to side so that they don't stick to the bottom of your fryer or pan.

Cook for 2–3 minutes, until crisp and brown and all over, then serve.

CHILLI CON CARNE

Every Boxing Day in my family I'm designated 'chilli maker'. I don't want to blow my own trumpet, but every person clears their plate! There's something about this warming dish that I crave weekly. I love it with a baked potato, or even added on top of my nachos (*see* page 66)!

SERVES 4

olive oil, for frying

2 garlic cloves, crushed or finely chopped

1 large onion, diced

1 teaspoon hot chilli powder

1 teaspoon ground cumin

1 teaspoon paprika

500 g (1 lb 2 oz) minced beef (any fat percentage)

1 red pepper, deseeded and diced

2 jalapeño chillies, diced

1 x 400 g (14 oz) can chopped tomatoes

2 heaped tablespoons tomato purée

1 gluten-free beef stock cube

1 x 400 g (14 oz) can red kidney beans in chilli sauce

Place a generous amount of olive oil in a large saucepan over a medium heat. When hot, add your garlic and onion and fry for 2 minutes.

Add your hot chilli powder, cumin and paprika and fry for another 2 minutes.

Now add your minced beef to the pan and allow it to brown, stirring now and then.

Once all your mince has browned, add your chopped pepper and chillies and cook for a further 2 minutes.

Add the chopped tomatoes and tomato purée, crumble in the stock cube and stir well.

Finally, add your red kidney beans in chilli sauce, lower the heat to a simmer and cook gently for a good 20 minutes.

Serve with fries or rice, or just add a sprinkling of grated cheese – whatever you fancy!

TEXAS CHICKEN

This mouth-watering chicken dish is another fave of mine, my go-to dish. Try it with my Paprika Potatoes and Mac & Cheese (*see* pages 74 and 77)!

SERVES 2

2 x 175 g (6 oz) chicken breast fillets

2 thick slices of Cheddar cheese (about 30 g/1 oz each)

4 strips of smoked bacon

1 tablespoon garlic granules

olive oil, for drizzling

gluten-free barbecue sauce

Preheat your oven to 180°C/160°C Fan (350°F), Gas Mark 4.

Using a sharp knife, slice into the side of each chicken breast to create a pocket for your filling.

Insert a slice of cheese into each pocket.

Starting 2.5 cm (1 in) from either end, wrap 2 strips of bacon around each chicken breast. This will hold the cheese in place.

Place the chicken breasts on a baking tray, sprinkle with the garlic granules and drizzle over some olive oil.

Roast for 20 minutes, then top each breast with a dollop of barbecue sauce and cook for a further 5 minutes.

ENCHILADAS

Spicy chicken in a warm tortilla pocket with melted cheese? It sounds like my perfect naughty night in dinner. I've always loved this style of food, and it's *sooo* easy to make, the perfect end to a busy day. You can always have a cheeky tequila cocktail with it too!

SERVES 4

olive oil, for frying

1 large onion, sliced

1 red pepper, deseeded and sliced

4 jalapeño chillies, sliced into rings

4 x 175 g (6 oz) chicken breast fillets, cut into bite-sized pieces

2 heaped teaspoons smoked paprika

½ teaspoon ground cumin

1 teaspoon garlic granules

1 teaspoon chilli flakes

4 gluten-free tortilla wraps

500 g (1 lb 2 oz) tomato passata

100g (3½ oz) Cheddar cheese, grated

sea salt flakes and pepper

Preheat your oven to 200°C/180°C Fan (400°F), Gas Mark 6.

Heat a generous splash of olive oil in a frying pan. When it's hot, add your onion and cook for 3–4 minutes.

Add your red pepper and sliced chillies and cook for another minute.

Add your chicken, then your smoked paprika, cumin, garlic granules, dried oregano and chilli flakes, and season with a large pinch of salt and pepper.

Cook until your chicken is coated in the spices and cooked through. This usually takes 8–10 minutes; you will know when it's ready!

Meanwhile, spread out your wraps in a baking tray. Fill them with your chicken mixture and roll each one into a tube shape. Lay the tubes beside each other in the tray and cover with your passata.

Sprinkle a generous amount of grated cheese over them – the more, the better for me! – and season with salt and pepper.

Place in the oven for 25 minutes, then serve.

PAPRIKA POTATOES

Crispy seasoned mini potatoes are a fave of mine. Crushing them little babies down and adding that paprika turns your baby potatoes into a mouthful of flavour. These pair well with chicken or steak and they're even great to enjoy with salads!

SERVES 2–4 AS A SIDE

400 g (14 oz) baby potatoes

olive oil, for drizzling

2 teaspoons paprika

1 heaped teaspoon garlic granules

sea salt flakes and pepper

Preheat your oven to 180°C/160°C Fan (350°F), Gas Mark 4.

Bring a large pan of water to the boil, then add your potatoes and cook for 25 minutes, or until tender.

Strain the potatoes and tip them into a large roasting tray.

Using a fork, push down on each potato, half-crushing them.

Drizzle the crushed potatoes with olive oil, making sure they are well coated.

Sprinkle over your paprika and garlic granules, then add a sprinkle of salt and a good crack of black pepper.

Place the tray in the oven for 40 minutes, turning the potatoes after 20 minutes so they are nice and crisp all over.

AMERICAN LETTUCE BURGER

I feel that with this recipe, a burger and other goodies sandwiched between lettuce leaves, you don't need a bun. The pickles and caramelized onion bring the burger together so well that bread is unnecessary, but you can add a GF bun if you really want to! Trust me when I tell you that lettuce burgers are the way forward. I like to serve these with my Southern Slaw (*see* page 76).

SERVES 4

450 g (1 lb) minced beef

1 tablespoon dried mixed herbs

1 tablespoon chilli flakes

1 teaspoon onion granules

3 large garlic cloves, crushed

1 egg

olive oil, for frying

2 large red onions, sliced

2 tablespoons white caster sugar

2 Baby Gem lettuce

2 tablespoons gluten-free tomato ketchup

2 tablespoons mayonnaise

4 square Cheddar cheese slices

2 large tomatoes, sliced

8 gherkins, sliced diagonally

salt and pepper

Place your minced beef in a bowl, add the dried herbs, chilli flakes, onion granules and garlic and mix well.

Crack in your egg and mix thoroughly with your hands. Season well with salt and pepper and mix again.

Divide the mixture into 4 equal pieces. Roll each piece into a ball, then flatten between your hands until roughly 3cm (1¼ in) thick. Set aside.

Heat a generous splash of olive oil in a frying pan. When hot, add your onions and sugar. Cook over a medium heat until the onions are soft and caramelized, stirring regularly until ready to serve.

Now it's time to cook your burgers. Heat some olive oil in a clean frying pan. When hot, add your burgers and cook for 7 minutes on each side.

While they're cooking, separate the lettuce leaves and place about 3 large ones on each serving plate. These, rather than buns, will act as the base for your burgers.

Combine your ketchup and mayonnaise in a small bowl, then spread some on the lettuce leaves where your burgers will sit.

About 2 minutes before the burgers are fully cooked, place a slice of cheese on each one, then cover the pan with a lid to help the cheese to melt.

Add a cheeseburger to the lettuce on each plate. Top with some sliced tomato, a few slices of gherkin and a big scoop of caramelized onions. Cover with another 2 or 3 lettuce leaves, if you like.

SOUTHERN SLAW

The perfect summer side dish!

SERVES 4 AS A SIDE

½ **head of red cabbage, finely shredded**

¼ **red onion, finely sliced**

115 g (4 oz) gluten-free **mayonnaise**

1 tablespoon gluten-free Dijon **mustard**

1½ tablespoons caster sugar

2 tablespoons apple cider **vinegar**

1 teaspoon onion powder

1 teaspoon celery salt

Place your cabbage and red onion in a sieve, pour over 500ml (18 fl oz) boiling water and set aside to drain for 5 minutes.

Meanwhile, place your mayonnaise in a large bowl with the mustard, sugar, vinegar, onion powder and celery salt and mix well.

Make sure your cabbage and onion are thoroughly drained, then add to the mayonnaise mixture. Stir well and serve.

MAC & CHEESE

One thing I always crave, even for breakfast, is mac & cheese. I love it! This GF version has a crunchy topping, a gooey middle and a lot of cheese. It's the perfect side for any meal, even with my Sirloin Steak (*see* page 87). Mix it up!

SERVES 4 AS A SIDE

2 teaspoons salt

1 tablespoon olive oil

325 g (11½ oz) gluten-free macaroni

400 g (14 oz) Cheddar cheese, grated

400 ml (14 fl oz) semi-skimmed milk

2 teaspoons pepper, plus extra for garnish

20 g (¾ oz) cornflour mixed with 2 tablespoons water

60 g (2¼ oz) gluten-free breadcrumbs

1 teaspoon garlic granules

Preheat your oven to 180°C/160°C Fan (350°F), Gas Mark 4. Set out a large baking dish, about 23 x 28 cm (9 x 11 in).

Bring a large pan of water to the boil and add 1 teaspoon of your salt along with your olive oil – this will help to prevent the pasta clumping together. Add your pasta and cook for 5 minutes; you don't want it fully cooked.

Meanwhile, place three-quarters of your cheese in a non-stick saucepan. Add the milk, then stir over a medium-high heat, until all the cheese has melted. Stir in your pepper and the remaining teaspoon of salt.

Now add your cornflour paste and stir for about 3 minutes, until the sauce thickens and the raw flour taste disappears.

Strain your pasta, return it to the pan and pour in your cheese sauce, stirring well.

Tip the mixture into your baking dish, sprinkle with your remaining cheese and cover with your breadcrumbs.

Season well with extra pepper and your garlic granules, then bake for 20 minutes!

MOZZARELLA BREADED CHICKEN WITH PESTO PASTA

There's nothing better than biting into chicken coated with crispy breadcrumbs, and that's something I can't say very often! This GF recipe lets us all enjoy the pleasures of the crunch alongside some delicious pesto pasta. I also love pairing this breaded chicken with my Mozzarella & Tomato Salad (*see* page 53)!

SERVES 2

100 g (3½ oz) gluten-free flour

4½ teaspoons salt

4 teaspoons black pepper

2 eggs

100 g (3½ oz) gluten-free breadcrumbs

2 x 175 g (6 oz) skinless chicken breast fillets

1 x 400 g (14 oz) can chopped tomatoes

1 tablespoon brown sugar

1 teaspoon dried oregano

250 ml (9 fl oz) vegetable oil

100 g (3½ oz) mozzarella cheese, cut into 6 slices

10 large basil leaves

4 tablespoons olive oil (optional)

Set out 3 wide, shallow bowls: place your flour in bowl 1 and season with 1 teaspoon of the salt and pepper; crack your eggs into bowl 2, add 1 teaspoon of the salt and pepper and whisk together with a fork; place your breadcrumbs in bowl 3 and season with 1 teaspoon of the salt and pepper.

Lay a sheet of clingfilm on a work surface, place your chicken breasts on it and cover with another sheet of clingfilm. Using a rolling pin, bash your chicken until it is butterflied, i.e. flattened out to about 5 mm (¼ in) thick.

Remove the clingfilm, then dip your chicken first into the flour bowl, then into your egg bowl, and finally into your breadcrumbs, making sure the meat is completely covered each time. Set aside!

Tip your tomatoes into a saucepan over a medium heat and add ½ teaspoon of the salt, 1 teaspoon of the pepper, the brown sugar and dried oregano. Stir well and bring to a simmer. Continue simmering for 20 minutes.

Meanwhile, place your vegetable oil in a deep frying pan over a medium heat. When the oil is hot, add your chicken breasts –

150 g (5½ oz) gluten-free spaghetti

3 teaspoons gluten-free basil pesto

1 tablespoon gluten-free balsamic glaze, to serve

depending on the size of your pan, you might have to cook them one at a time – and fry over a medium-high heat for 3 minutes on each side.

Heat your grill until very hot. Bring a large pan of water to the boil.

Transfer the chicken to a baking dish and spoon your tomato sauce over it. Top each piece with 3 mozzarella slices and 2 large basil leaves, then place under your hot grill for 10 minutes or until the cheese is molten and golden.

Add 2 tablespoons of your olive oil, if you like, and the remaining teaspoon of salt to the boiling water and cook the spaghetti for 9 minutes.

Drain the pasta, reserving 2 tablespoons of the water. Return the pasta to the empty pan and stir in your pesto, adding the reserved pasta water or the remaining 2 tablespoons olive oil if it seems dry.

Serve the chicken topped with the remaining fresh basil and a drizzle of balsamic glaze, and with your pesto pasta on the side.

COTTAGE PIE

Who doesn't love a homemade cottage pie? Over the years, this has been one of my favourite dishes to cook, and it's full of goodness. Using all GF alternatives, I have created the tastiest version you will ever try!

SERVES 4 ———————————————————————————————

1.5 kg (3 lb 5 oz) floury potatoes, peeled and cut into eighths

70 g (2½ oz) salted butter

100 ml (3½ fl oz) milk

3 carrots, peeled and sliced

olive oil, for frying

1 large onion, finely diced

500 g (1 lb 2 oz) minced beef (12% fat)

2 gluten-free beef stock cubes

2 tablespoons beef gravy granules

1 tablespoon gluten-free soy sauce

4 tablespoons gluten-free Worcestershire sauce

140 g (5 oz) frozen peas

140 g (5 oz) frozen sweetcorn kernels

1 x 400 g (14 oz) can chopped tomatoes

1 tablespoon chilli flakes

Preheat your oven to 180°C/160°C Fan (350°F), Gas Mark 4. Set out a 23 x 28 cm (9 x 11 in) ovenproof dish.

To make your mashed potato to go on top of the pie, bring a large pan of water to the boil and season with a generous pinch of salt.

Add your potatoes and cook over a medium-high heat for 20 minutes. In the meantime, make the filling.

Place your carrots in a pan of boiling water and cook for about 10–15 minutes, until partly soft.

Pour a splash of olive oil into a large frying pan and cook your onion for 2–3 minutes until slightly softened.

Add your beef along with a generous pinch of salt and pepper, and cook until it begins to brown.

Now crumble in your stock cubes and add your beef gravy granules, soy sauce and Worcestershire sauce, and cook until your mince has completely browned.

Stir in your peas, sweetcorn, tomatoes and chilli flakes.

Strain your carrots and add to your beef mixture, being careful not to break them! Allow to simmer over a low heat while you finish your mashed potatoes.

Make sure your potatoes are cooked – they're ready when the point of a knife pierces them easily. Strain the potatoes into a sieve, then return them to the empty saucepan and add your butter and half your milk.

Mash your potatoes, then add the remainder of your milk and a generous amount of black pepper. Make sure to mash until all the lumps have disappeared.

Pour your beef mixture into your ovenproof dish, then carefully spoon your mashed potato on top, spreading it out and leaving no gaps. Fluff the surface with a fork.

Place in the oven for 45 minutes, until golden brown on top.

I like to serve my pie with extra gravy (made with 2 tablespoons gluten-free beef gravy granules) and fresh vegetables – the perfect comfort dinner!

SIRLOIN STEAK

I have always been a fillet steak kinda girl, but then I discovered the sirloin! It's all about how you cook it – crispy on the outside but tender in the middle. Make sure you pair this with my Blue Cheese Sauce and Triple-Cooked Chips (*see* pages 91 and 90). The best!

SERVES 2

2 x 200 g (7 oz) sirloin steaks

30 g (1 oz) butter

juice of ½ lemon

sea salt flakes

Season your steaks generously on both sides with salt.

Melt your butter in a large frying pan over a high heat until golden brown and frothy.

Add your steaks to the pan and leave to cook, without moving them, for about 2 minutes. Flip them over and cook the other side for 2 minutes, browning the corners by moving them around for a few seconds. This timing cooks the steaks medium-rare, which I think is the best way to enjoy them.

Squeeze your lemon juice over the steaks and use a spoon to baste them with your butter!

Transfer to a board or plate and rest for 10 minutes so that the juices are reabsorbed by the meat. This ensures that your steaks are tender but won't bleed on the plate.

Slice the rested steaks and serve them with your chosen accompaniments.

TRIPLE-COOKED CHIPS

You'd be surprised how much of a difference triple cooking chips can make. It's all about getting that seasoned crunchy layer on the outside and fluffiness in the middle. Once you try these bad boys, you won't ever cook normal fries again. You can serve these with anything or eat them on their own, but please try them with my steak and blue cheese sauce... they're a must!

SERVES 4 AS A SIDE

5 large floury potatoes (about 1.5 kg/3 lb 5 oz), peeled

1.5 litres (52 fl oz) rapeseed oil, for deep-frying

sea salt flakes

Bring a large pan of water to the boil.

Cut your potatoes into chips measuring about 8 x 2 x 2 cm (3¼ x ¾ x ¾ in).

Place the chips in a large sieve and rinse under running cold water to remove the excess starch. This usually takes 1–2 minutes.

Add a generous pinch of salt to your water, then boil the chips for about 15 minutes, until a fork goes in without breaking them.

Strain your chips into a sieve. You may notice they look fluffy around the edges, which is good! If your chips don't have those fluffy edges, give them a gentle shake.

Place the chips one at a time on a wire rack and gently pat dry with kitchen paper. Pop them into the refrigerator to completely cool (or even into the freezer if you want to speed things up). The first stage of your triple-cooked chips is now complete.

Once the chips have cooled completely, season well with salt.

Pour the oil into a deep-fat fryer and heat to 160°C (325°F) degrees. Alternatively, pour the oil into a deep saucepan, filling it no more than one-third full, and heat until a cube of bread browns in 40–45 seconds. Once the oil is hot enough, add a small batch of your chips and cook for 8 minutes. (Be careful not to overcrowd the basket or you'll lower the temperature of the oil too much and your chips won't cook properly.) Drain the cooked chips on kitchen paper, then cook the remainder in the same way. The second stage is now complete.

Allow the chips to cool, then heat the oil again to 180°C (350°F), or until a cube of bread browns in 30–40 seconds.

Place a small batch of chips back in the hot oil and cook for a further 2½ minutes. Drain on kitchen paper and keep warm while you cook the remaining chips in the same way.

Season your chips with salt and enjoy.

BLUE CHEESE SAUCE

This sauce goes brilliantly with my Sirloin Steaks (*see* page 87).

SERVES 4 AS A SIDE

150 g (5½ oz) blue cheese, such as Roquefort or Stilton

50 ml (2 fl oz) double cream

1 teaspoon cornflour mixed with 2 tablespoons water

Place your cheese in a saucepan over a low-medium heat and allow it to melt.

Stir in your cream and simmer for 1 minute.

Add the cornflour liquid to your cheese sauce, stir well and simmer for 2–3 minutes.

ARANCINI

These crunchy breaded rice balls, deep fried and dipped in a chilli sauce, are a little pop of heaven. Stop! Why can't restaurants provide this sort of dish for us GF people? These melting-middle balls are the best dinner party starter, and also go great with pre-dinner party drinks! Serve with my Chilli Dip (*see* page 95).

MAKES ABOUT 12

375 ml (12 fl oz) gluten-free chicken stock

60 g (2¼ oz) unsalted butter

½ onion, diced

1 garlic clove, crushed

125 g (4½ oz) carnaroli rice

¼ teaspoon salt

60 ml (2 fl oz) dry white wine

125 g (4½ oz) Parmesan cheese, grated

2 tablespoons double cream

zest of 1 lemon

½ tablespoon lemon juice

½ teaspoon black pepper

125 g (4½ oz) mozzarella cheese, cut into 12 equal pieces

30 g (1 oz) gluten-free plain flour

Bring your stock to a simmer in a saucepan, then keep warm over a very low heat.

Melt half your butter in a separate pan, then fry your onion for 4 minutes, until slightly softened. Add your garlic and fry for 1 minute.

Stir in your rice and salt, and cook for about 3 minutes, stirring often, until the grains start to become translucent. It's really important to keep stirring so your rice doesn't stick!

Add your wine and stir for about 2 minutes, until the pan is almost dry.

Now add a cupful of your warm stock and continue cooking and stirring until most of the liquid is absorbed; this will take about 4 minutes. Continue adding the stock a cupful at a time, allowing each addition to be almost fully absorbed before adding the next. When all the stock has been used, the risotto should be moist but not loose, with al dente grains.

Take the pan off the heat and stir in your Parmesan, cream, lemon zest and juice, the black pepper and your remaining butter.

1 large egg, beaten

200 g (7 oz) gluten-free breadcrumbs

rapeseed or vegetable oil, for deep-frying

Spread your risotto evenly in a baking tray, cover with clingfilm and set aside to cool for 1 hour. Transfer to the refrigerator and leave until completely chilled.

Set out another baking tray. Scoop a heaped tablespoon of the chilled risotto into your hand, place a piece of mozzarella in the centre, then press the risotto around it to form a ball about the size of a golf ball. The mixture should make around 12 balls.

Place the balls in the empty baking tray, then freeze for 10 minutes. Meanwhile, set out another baking tray and line it with non-stick baking paper.

Grab three bowls and put your flour in one, your beaten egg in another, and your breadcrumbs in the third. Season each bowl with salt and pepper.

Dip each arancini first in the flour, shaking off any excess, then coat well in the egg, and finally roll in the breadcrumbs. Transfer to your prepared baking tray and chill until you're ready to cook the arancini.

Fill a deep-fat fryer with oil and heat to 180°C (350°F) degrees. Alternatively, pour the oil into a deep saucepan, filling it no more than one-third full, and heat until a cube of bread browns in 40–45 seconds.

Using a slotted spoon, carefully lower half the arancini into the hot oil and cook for 7 minutes, until golden brown and crisp all over. Drain on kitchen paper , season with a little salt, if you like, and transfer to a serving plate. Cooking the remaining arancini in the same way.

CHILLI DIP

Now if you like a bit of extra zing, then this recipe is for you – a light spicy dip for your arancini balls (*see* pages 93–4) or breaded chicken (see page 81). Whatever you wanna dip in it, this finishes off your tasting bites perfectly and is SO easy to make.

SERVES 2–4

1 red bird's eye chilli (this is very hot), finely diced

2 mild red chillies, finely diced

½ garlic clove, finely diced

½ teaspoon lemon zest

2 teaspoons lemon juice

2 tablespoons extra virgin olive oil

Place your chillies and garlic in a bowl.

Add your lemon zest, lemon juice and olive oil and mix well.

Cover tightly with clingfilm and place in the refrigerator to chill until ready to serve.

FROZEN MARGARITA

The go-to frozen cocktail for me is a margarita! The glass usually has salt around the rim, but I like to have sugar. There's something about this drink that makes me feel so refreshed and fancy! And for me, tequila means no bad hangover, so it's a winner!

SERVES 1

2 cups ice

50ml (2 fl oz) gold tequila

25ml (1 fl oz) Cointreau

juice of 2 limes

50ml (2 fl oz) sugar syrup (*see* page 100)

fine salt or sugar, for the rim of the glass

lime slices, to serve

If your ice is in large pieces, give it a little bash to break them down slightly.

Place the ice in your blender, then pour in your tequila, Cointreau, lime juice and sugar syrup and blend until the liquid has a slush-like consistency.

Grab a large plate and spread an even layer of salt or sugar on it, whichever you prefer.

Pour a little of the cocktail mixture into a saucer. Dip the rim of your cocktail glass into the liquid, then dip it into the salt or sugar – this will create that iconic margarita edge.

Fill your glass carefully with the frozen cocktail, making sure not to ruin that edge. Add a slice lime and drink up!

PICANTE

Tequila is truly my social saviour. Feeling tipsy with no hangover is the perfect combo, right? This spiced cocktail is my favourite on a night out. Make sure it's over ice, and don't be eating the chilli garnish if you've had a few too many, ha!

SERVES 1

2 red chillies, 1 finely chopped, 1 left whole

2 shots reposado tequila (this type has been aged for up to 12 months in oak)

2 sprigs fresh coriander

1 shot agave syrup or sugar syrup (*see* page 100)

3 shots fresh lime juice

½ shot soda water

1 cup large ice cubes

Place your chopped chilli in a cocktail shaker.

Add your tequila, coriander, syrup and lime juice. Shake well, then add your soda water.

Fill a short glass with your ice and strain your picante over the top. Garnish with your whole chilli.

PORN STAR MARTINI

This is my family's secret recipe! I have tried many porn stars in my time (don't take that the wrong way!) and this recipe beats them all. It's smooth and sweet, the perfect pre-dinner drink, and always looks cute for Insta. Cheers!

SERVES 1

1 cup ice

50 ml (2 fl oz) vanilla vodka (make sure it's gluten-free)

25 ml (1 fl oz) peach schnapps

100 ml (3½ fl oz) passion fruit juice

50 ml (2 fl oz) sugar syrup (*see* Tip below)

½ passion fruit

25 ml (1 fl oz) Prosecco (optional – make sure it's gluten-free)

Place the ice in your cocktail shaker and add the vodka, schnapps, passion fruit juice and sugar syrup.

Put the lid on firmly, and shake well until the mixture is a little frothy.

Pour into a cocktail glass of your choice and garnish with the passion fruit half.

The cocktail is now ready to serve, but you can add a shot of Prosecco if you like, provided it's gluten-free!

TIP

How to make sugar syrup

Although you can buy bottles of sugar syrup, it's very easy to make your own. Place 300g (10½ oz) caster sugar in a saucepan with 150 ml (5 fl oz) water and stir over a low heat until the sugar has completely dissolved. Allow to cool for 5 minutes, then pour into a sterilized bottle and seal tightly. Sugar syrup will keep for up to six months in the fridge.

FROZEN STRAWBERRY DAIQUIRI

I always feel I'm on holiday when drinking my famous daiquiri. It looks so impressive and the icy slush tastes so nice that you forget you're drinking alcohol! So be careful, people, these can be dangerous!

SERVES 1

2 cups ice

75 ml (2½ fl oz) white rum

50 ml (2 fl oz) sugar syrup (*see* page 100)

juice of 2 limes

160 g (5¾ oz) strawberries, hulled and halved, plus extra for garnish

If your ice is in large pieces, give it a little bash to break them down slightly.

Place the ice in your blender, then pour in your white rum, sugar syrup and lime juice. Add your strawberries and blend until everything's nice and smooth.

Pour into a cocktail glass of your choice and add a strawberry to the rim of the glass to garnish.

'Yes, I'm gluten-free and wheat-free.'
'Yes, it's an allergy.'
'Yes, coeliac disease.'

'NO, I DON'T WANT A SALAD!'

POSH NOSH

SCALLOPS WITH CHILLI
PEA PURÉE

MINI BEEF
WELLINGTONS

GARLIC-SAUTÉD GREEN
BEANS

RED WINE JUS

DAUPHINOISE
POTATOES

CHAMPAGNE CHICKEN

HOT TOMATO SPINACH

CHICKEN CHASSEUR

BEEF & ROASTIES

CHESTNUT & BACON
BRUSSELS SPROUTS

HONEY & CHILLI-
GLAZED CARROTS

CAULIFLOWER CHEESE

CURRIED COD

ONION BHAJIS

CAULIFLOWER
PURÉE

LAMB SHANKS

CREAMY MASHED
POTATOES

PARMESAN RISOTTO
WITH GARLIC
PRAWNS

LOBSTER RAVIOLI
IN VODKA SAUCE

POSH NOSH

Ooooh, now this is where it gets really fancy. Posh nosh is my favourite food ever!

I love to cook for people, but my party trick is to make a three-course meal, let my guests demolish the lot, and then tell them it was all gluten-free. Believe me, I have had many shocked faces at the table!

I'm not kidding you when I say the recipes in this chapter are freakin' amazing. Great food is put together with love, but the most important element is flavour, and you'll find plenty of that here, from creamy chicken dishes to mini Beef Wellingtons. I have also included all my favourite sides, from honey-glazed chilli carrots to cauliflower cheese, which I make as part of my famous roast dinners that I post on my socials once a week. (My amazing mum taught me how when I left home, and her roasts are the best!) How annoying is it when you go to someone's house for a roast and you can only have the boring bits? *I want it all*, and now you can have it too!

Now it's time to grab a glass of whatever floats your boat, whack on that apron and get stuck into these divine recipes.

SCALLOPS WITH CHILLI PEA PURÉE

I enjoy eating scallops when I'm out for dinner, but they always seem to lack something. Now I've worked out what it is – spice! Adding chilli to seafood has made them one of my faves. Your guests won't be disappointed with this cute dish.

SERVES 4

90 g (3¼ oz) salted butter

1 garlic clove, finely chopped

2 bird's eye chillies, finely chopped

400 g (14 oz) frozen peas

50 ml (2 fl oz) double cream

1 lemon

1 parsnip, shaved into lengthways strips

8 slices of pancetta

4 tablespoons honey

4 large scallops

salt and pepper

Preheat your oven to 180°C/160°C Fan (350°F), Gas Mark 4.

Place half your butter in a large deep pan over a medium heat and allow to melt.

Add your garlic, chillies and peas and cook for 2–3 minutes.

Now add your cream, season with salt and pepper and stir well.

Using a hand blender, blitz the mixture until smooth. Add a squeeze of lemon juice, then blitz again to combine.

Arrange your parsnips and pancetta on a baking tray, drizzle with honey and season well. Roast for 15–20 minutes, until crisp.

Place the remaining butter in a frying pan over a high heat. When nice and hot, add your scallops and sear for about 2–3 minutes on each side, until golden (the time depends on the size of your scallops).

I like to serve this recipe in bowls with a small, deep centre. Place 2 tablespoons of the pea purée in the bottom, then sit the scallops on it.

Add a squeeze of lemon juice and arrange the roasted parsnips and pancetta on top.

MINI BEEF WELLINGTONS

Isn't it refreshing to see a pastry-based dish on the menu? Beef Wellingtons are top of my list for posh nosh dinners, and pair perfectly with my Dauphinoise Potatoes, Garlic Sautéd Green beans and Red Wine Jus (*see* pages 116, 114 and 115). The tender beef alongside that lovely combination of flavours makes me so happy!

SERVES 2

500 g (1 lb 2 oz) fillet of beef

olive oil, for searing

300 g (10½ oz) closed cup white mushrooms, roughly chopped

8 slices of Parma ham

1 x 280 g (10 oz) packet ready-rolled gluten-free puff pastry

1 egg, beaten

salt and pepper

Preheat your oven to 200°C/180°C Fan (400°F), Gas Mark 6.

Season your beef well with salt and pepper, then slice in half widthways to make 2 fillets.

Pour a splash of olive oil into a frying pan over a medium-high heat. When hot, add the beef and sear on all sides until golden brown. Transfer to a plate and set aside to cool.

Place your mushrooms in a blender and blitz until finely chopped.

Pour a splash of olive oil into your empty frying pan, add the mushrooms and season well. Cook for about 7 minutes, until softened.

Place a large sheet of clingfilm on a clean work surface, then place 4 of the ham slices on it in a single layer, overlapping them so that there are no gaps. Prepare a second sheet of clingfilm and ham in the same way. Now spoon your mushrooms evenly over both sheets of ham.

Sit a beef fillet on each sheet of ham, then use the clingfilm to help you lift and roll the ham around each one until it is tightly enclosed. Twist the ends of the clingfilm to keep the parcels rolled up. Place in in the fridge until chilled to the touch.

Unroll the pastry on your work surface, leaving it on the paper it's wrapped in and cut in half widthways.

Remove the clingfilm, then place a ham-wrapped beef fillet close to the short edge of a piece of pastry. Brush around the other 3 edges with your beaten egg. Roll the pastry around the beef and press the eggy edges together to seal. Repeat this step with the other beef fillet.

Brush both pastry parcels with beaten egg, then transfer to a baking tray and place in the oven for 25 minutes, until the pastry is flaky and golden.

GARLIC-SAUTÉD GREEN BEANS

The perfect accompaniment to any meal!

SERVES 2–4 AS A SIDE

75 g (2¾ oz) salted butter

200 g (7 oz) French green beans, trimmed

1 tablespoon garlic granules

pepper

Place your butter in a pan over a medium-high heat.

When the butter has melted, add your green beans and cook for 5 minutes, stirring now and then.

Season generously with pepper, then cook for a further 5 minutes, until the beans are al dente.

Transfer to a serving bowl and sprinkle with your garlic granules.

RED WINE JUS

The perfect accompaniment to my mini Beef Wellingtons (*see* page 112)!

SERVES 2–4

olive oil, for frying

1 onion, finely diced

1 tablespoon caster sugar

750 ml (27 fl oz) red wine

400 ml (14 fl oz) hot gluten-free vegetable stock

2 bay leaves

2 sprigs of rosemary

2 sprigs of thyme

1 tablespoon garlic granules

30 g (1 oz) salted butter

3 tablespoons cornflour

salt and pepper

Heat a splash of olive oil in a saucepan.

When hot, add the onion, season with salt and pepper, then add your sugar. Cook the onions over a medium-low heat, until they caramelize. This usually takes about 10 minutes.

Add your wine and allow it to reduce by half over a medium-high heat.

Pour in your stock, then add the herbs and garlic granules and season lightly with salt and pepper. Leave to reduce by half again.

Once the sauce has reduced, strain through a sieve into a clean saucepan over a medium heat.

Add your butter and cornflour, give it a good stir, and cook for 2–3 minutes until it's nice and thick. That's it!

DAUPHINOISE POTATOES

A dish full of cream and garlic? You can't go wrong really! This is such a great side to add to any posh nosh dinner! I love the texture of the soft potatoes in the cream sauce. It's so good I could eat a bowl of it on its own.

SERVES 4 AS A SIDE

1 kg (2 lb 4 oz) large floury potatoes, peeled and thinly sliced

400 ml (14 fl oz) double cream

2 garlic cloves, crushed or finely chopped

salt and pepper

Preheat your oven to 180°C/160° Fan (350°F), Gas Mark 4. Set out a 23 x 15 cm (9 x 6 in) ovenproof dish.

Arrange an even layer of potato slices in your dish and season with salt and pepper.

Repeat this layering process until you've used all your potato slices.

Combine the cream and garlic in a bowl or jug and mix well.

Pour this mixture over your potatoes and season once again with salt and pepper.

Bake for about 45 minutes, until golden and bubbly.

CHAMPAGNE CHICKEN

If you're hosting a dinner party, stop right here! This is the perfect dish to cook and will impress your whole party. Add my Hot Tomato Spinach side dish (*see* page 120) and your choice of potatoes, and you won't be disappointed. Don't forget to serve with a tall glass of champagne!

SERVES 2

2 chicken legs, with skin

60 g (2¼ oz) salted butter

olive oil

1 large onion, finely chopped

150 g (5½ oz) button mushrooms, sliced

2 tablespoons brandy

225 ml (8 fl oz) gluten-free chicken stock

150 ml (5 fl oz) champagne

½ teaspoon dried thyme

1 bay leaf

2 teaspoons cornflour

165 ml (5½ fl oz) double cream

salt and pepper

Preheat your oven to 180°C/160°C Fan (350°F), Gas Mark 4.

Season your chicken legs with salt and pepper.

Place half your butter in a frying pan over a medium heat and add a splash of olive oil. When the butter has melted, add the chicken legs and sear them for about 10 minutes, until golden brown.

Transfer the chicken legs to a roasting tray and roast for 20–25 minutes, until cooked through.

Meanwhile, melt your remaining butter in the frying pan over a medium heat. Add your onion and mushrooms and cook until softened.

Pour in the brandy, chicken stock and champagne, then add the thyme and bay leaf.

Sprinkle the cornflour into the mixture, stir vigorously to combine, then leave to simmer for a few minutes.

Add your double cream, along with salt and pepper to taste, and leave to simmer until the chicken is ready.

Pour the sauce over the chicken to serve.

HOT TOMATO SPINACH

This is no Popeye spinach. This side is so tasty and complements your posh nosh dishes perfectly. Hot wilted spinach, seasoned well, with tomatoes that burst in your mouth – it works amazingly together! I highly recommend it.

SERVES 2–4 AS A SIDE

olive oil, for frying

1 garlic clove, finely chopped

1 x 250 g (9 oz) pack cherry tomatoes

300 g (10½ oz) fresh spinach

1 teaspoon chilli flakes

sea salt flakes and pepper

Pour a splash of olive oil into a large saucepan over a medium-high heat. When hot, add your garlic and cook for about 1 minute.

Add your tomatoes to the pan, gently stirring to coat them evenly in the garlic oil. Cook until lightly browned and beginning to split. This usually takes about 8 minutes.

Now add your spinach – you might need to add half at first and allow it to wilt down so you can fit in the rest. As the spinach shrinks, you will notice it begins to soften and turn dark green.

Season with a sprinkle of salt, a generous amount of black pepper and your chilli flakes. Be sure to use a straining spoon when serving so that any excess liquid is left in the pan.

CHICKEN CHASSEUR

My go-to winter dinner – I love the red wine-based sauce – this one went down well on my socials. It's so tasty that you won't want to stop eating it. Serve with my Creamy Mashed Potatoes and Garlic Sautéd Green Beans (*see* pages 137 and 114) for a perfect cosy night in!

SERVES 4

60 g (2¼ oz) salted butter

olive oil, for frying

1 large onion, roughly chopped

3 garlic cloves, roughly chopped

200 g (7 oz) baby button mushrooms, finely sliced

350 ml (12 fl oz) red wine (I use a fruity, jammy red)

2 sprigs of fresh thyme, or 2 tablespoons dried thyme

3 tablespoons tomato purée

500 ml (18 fl oz) hot gluten-free chicken stock

3 x 225 g (8 oz) chicken breast fillets, skin on

2 tablespoons cornflour mixed with 5 tablespoons cold water

salt and pepper

Place half the butter and 2 tablespoons olive oil in a large saucepan over a medium heat. Once the butter has melted, add your onion and garlic and fry for about 5 minutes, until partly softened.

Add your mushrooms and cook for 1 minute, then pour in your red wine and turn the heat up to medium-high. Allow the wine to reduce by about a third so that the alcohol evaporates. This usually takes about 10 minutes.

Once your wine has reduced, add your thyme and tomato purée. Mix well, then add the remaining butter and season generously with pepper.

Pour in your stock and leave to simmer over a low heat for 20 minutes.

Meanwhile, cut your chicken into small chunks and season with salt and pepper.

Place 1 tablespoon olive oil in a frying pan over a medium heat. When hot, add the chicken and cook thoroughly, ensuring it's white all the way through. This will take 10–15 minutes.

Add the chicken to the fully simmered sauce, then pour in your cornflour liquid. Turn the heat up to medium and stir for a couple of minutes, until the sauce thickens.

BEEF & ROASTIES

A traditional roast dinner has been part of my family for generations. Every Sunday we all sit down and have a feast. Beef and roast potatoes are my fave! Make sure you add all my side dishes to make the ultimate roast dinner (*see* pages 125–130). The carrots and cauliflower are insane!

SERVES 4

5 large floury potatoes (about 1.5kg/3 lb 5 oz), peeled and chopped into eighths and sixths (for a bit of variety)

1 x 1.1 kg (2 lb 10 oz) beef roasting joint

olive oil, for drizzling

2 sprigs of rosemary, leaves chopped

2 sprigs of thyme, plus 1 tablespoon leaves for sprinkling

salt and pepper

Preheat your oven to 190°C/170°C Fan (375°F), Gas Mark 5.

Bring a large pan of water to the boil. Add a pinch of salt, then cook your potatoes over a medium-high heat for 15–20 minutes, until slightly softened.

Meanwhile, place your beef in a roasting tray, drizzle with olive oil and season well with salt and pepper. Rub the chopped rosemary over the meat for extra flavour, sit the thyme sprigs on top, then roast for 50 minutes.

Strain the par-boiled potatoes into a sieve and give them a good shake to make sure they get those fluffy edges. This is what makes your roasties crisp on the outside and fluffy in the middle.

Transfer them to a large roasting tray with a generous drizzle of olive oil, turning them to coat thoroughly. Sprinkle with salt, the thyme leaves and pepper. Roast for about 50 minutes – the crispier the better in my opinion.

Remove the beef from the oven, cover loosely with foil and set aside to rest for 25 minutes. The resting process is really important as it allows the juices to be reabsorbed by the meat.

By the time the beef has finished resting, the potatoes should be done. Serve with your side dishes for the perfect Sunday lunch!

CHESTNUT & BACON BRUSSELS SPROUTS

I've never been a boring veg type of girl. Mixing things up with salty bacon and crunchy chestnuts makes your Brussels that little bit more special and creates so much flavour. This definitely is an impressive side dish for your guests!

SERVES 4

4 tablespoons olive oil

300 g (10½ oz) bag of Brussels sprouts, sliced into halves or thirds, depending on size

1 heaped tablespoon garlic granules

160 g (5¾ oz) bacon lardons

100 g (3½ oz) ready-cooked chestnuts

sea salt flakes and pepper

Place your olive oil in a large pan over a medium heat. When the oil is hot, add your sprouts and cook for 4 minutes, turning now and then.

Add a large splash of water and let it bubble away until evaporated.

Sprinkle in your garlic granules, then add your lardons and cook for 5 minutes, until crisp.

Now crumble in your chestnuts and mix them in.

Add 2 pinches of salt and a generous crack of pepper.

HONEY & CHILLI-GLAZED CARROTS

You can thank me later for this one!

SERVES 4 AS A SIDE

200 g (7 oz) whole carrots, trimmed

olive oil, for drizzling

honey, for drizzling

chilli flakes

salt and pepper

Preheat your oven to 180°C/160°C Fan (350°F), Gas Mark 4.

Lay out your carrots in a roasting tray and drizzle olive oil all over them.

Now generously drizzle them with honey and sprinkle with chilli flakes, as many as you like. Season well with salt and pepper.

Roast for 45–50 minutes, until tender and sticky.

CAULIFLOWER CHEESE

For most of my life, this was the side dish I wanted but could never have. Now, though, I've made this GF version, and it's so easy that you will bang out cauliflower cheese three times a week, haha!

SERVES 4 AS A SIDE

1 x 550 g (1 lb 4 oz) cauliflower, chopped into small florets

200 g (7 oz) medium-strong Cheddar cheese

300 ml (10 fl oz) semi-skimmed milk

2 tablespoons cornflour

salt and pepper

Preheat your oven to 180°C/160°C Fan (350°F), Gas Mark 4. Set out a deep ovenproof dish, about 20 x 20 cm (8 x 8 in).

Bring a large pan of water to the boil. Add a large pinch of salt, then add the cauliflower and cook for about 10 minutes – you want it slightly firm, not soft and soggy!

Meanwhile, grate your Cheddar into a saucepan, add the the milk and stir over a medium heat until smooth.

Place the cornflour in a mug, add a splash of cold water and mix to a smooth paste. Stir this into your cheese mixture to thicken it into a sauce. If you prefer it thicker, just add more cornflour paste.

Strain the cauliflower well and tip it into your ovenproof dish.

Pour the cheese sauce over the cauliflower and season with salt and pepper.

Pop the dish into the oven for 30 minutes, until all golden and bubbling.

CURRIED COD

Curry powder is one of my favourite spices, and goes beautifully with flaky fresh cod. This dish tastes insane with my Cauliflower Purée and Onion Bhajis (*see* pages 135 and 134) – another showstopper to serve your guests!

SERVES 2

2 x 120g (4 oz) cod fillets

olive oil, for frying

1 tablespoon mild curry powder

100 g (3½ oz) butter

juice of 1 lemon

15 g (½ oz) fresh coriander, leaves picked

salt

edible flowers of your choice, to garnish (optional)

Preheat your oven to 180°C/160°C Fan (350°F), Gas Mark 4.

Season your cod fillets with salt.

Place a non-stick, ovenproof frying pan over a medium-high heat and add a dash of olive oil. When hot, cook the cod for 2 minutes, then transfer to the oven for 5 minutes.

Remove from the oven and add your curry powder and butter. Place over a medium heat. Once the butter becomes foamy, use a spoon to baste the fish for 2 minutes.

Squeeze over the lemon juice, then sprinkle with the coriander and a pinch of salt.

Garnish with your edible flowers (if using) before serving.

ONION BHAJIS

Deep-fried bhajis make an amazing side dish. The crunchy outside and soft onion middle are to die for! These GF balls of goodness take just minutes to make, so what's stopping you! I would pair them with my Curried Cod (*see* page 133).

MAKES 8

vegetable oil, for shallow-frying

80 g (2¾ oz) gluten-free plain flour (I use gram/chickpea flour)

70 g (2½ oz) cornflour

2 teaspoons medium-hot curry powder

100 ml (3½ fl oz) cold water

2 onions, finely sliced

10 g (¼ oz) fresh coriander, roughly chopped

2.5 cm (1 in) piece fresh ginger, peeled and grated

2 garlic cloves, grated

sea salt flakes

The bhajis can be cooked in a frying pan or a deep-fat fryer. If using a fryer, fill it with oil and preheat it to 160°C (325°F).

Place your flour in a large bowl along with your cornflour, curry powder and a generous pinch of salt.

Stir in the measured water and mix well until you have a smooth, thick batter.

Add your onions, coriander, ginger and garlic, and mix gently until the onions are thoroughly coated.

If you're shallow-frying, add enough oil to fill a deep pan just under a quarter of its depth. Place over a medium heat for about 5 minutes. It is hot enough for frying when a tiny drop of batter rises to the surface surrounded by bubbles and begins to brown.

Once the oil has reached the correct temperature, use 2 tablespoons to make generous scoops of your bhaji mixture and carefully lower them into the hot oil. Fry for 5–7 minutes, until they float to the surface and are golden brown. If shallow-frying, turn them over after 3 minutes so both sides are evenly cooked. Lift out with a slotted spoon and drain on kitchen paper.

Serve with a sprinkle of sea salt flakes and enjoy!

CAULIFLOWER PURÉE

I think this purée is the best you can get. Add a swipe of it across the plate when you want to be fancy with your roast, or serve it alongside a fish dish. This works in so many ways that it takes almost any dish to another level.

SERVES 2 —————————————————————————————

100 g (3½ oz) butter

1 teaspoon ground ginger

1½ teaspoons cumin seeds

1 garlic clove, finely chopped

2 tablespoons medium-hot curry powder

1 x 500 g (1 lb 2 oz) cauliflower, roughly chopped

250 ml (9 fl oz) milk

250 ml (9 fl oz) double cream

50 g (1¾ oz) good-quality mango chutney

juice of ½ lemon

salt

Melt the butter in a pan, then add your ginger, cumin seeds, garlic and curry powder. Stir well and cook for 5 minutes over a medium heat.

Add your cauliflower to the spices, season well with salt and cook for 5 minutes, until it begins to soften.

Add your milk and simmer over a low heat until the cauliflower is tender.

Add your cream and simmer until the liquid has reduced and thickened.

Transfer the contents of the pan to a blender, add the mango chutney and lemon juice, and blitz until smooth. For extra smoothness, press the purée through a fine sieve using the back of a spoon.

If you're feeling fancy when it comes to serving, pour the purée into a squeezy bottle and create patterns on each plate, or squeeze out a small amount and push a spoon across it to make a fan shape.

LAMB SHANKS

I hope you've got a few dinner parties or a cute dinner for two lined up soon because this dish is begging for you to make it! The longer you cook the meat, the more tender it becomes, until it literally falls off the bone! Serve with whatever veg you like, but be sure to include my Creamy Mashed Potatoes to soak up that lovely wine sauce. Yum!

SERVES 4

olive oil, for frying

4 lamb shanks, or use just 2 if you want them to be extra saucy

3 garlic cloves, finely chopped

1 onion, roughly chopped

4 carrots, peeled and chopped

4 celery sticks, chopped

630 ml (21 fl oz) red wine

6 sprigs of fresh thyme or 1 tablespoon dried thyme

2 dried bay leaves

500 ml (18 fl oz) gluten-free chicken stock

2 tablespoons tomato purée

2 x 400 g (14 oz) cans chopped tomatoes

salt and pepper

Preheat your oven to 180°C/160°C Fan (350°F), Gas Mark 4.

Place 2 tablespoons olive oil in a large frying pan over a medium heat.

Meanwhile, season your lamb shanks with salt and pepper. Add them to the hot oil and sear on each side for about 4 minutes, until nice and golden. Transfer to a roasting tray and set aside.

Add another 2 tablespoons olive oil to the frying pan and cook your garlic and onion for about 2 minutes.

Add your carrots and celery and cook, stirring now and then, for a further 5 minutes.

Now it's time to add your wine, thyme and bay leaves. Stir well, then leave to cook over a medium heat for 5 minutes.

Add your stock, tomato purée and tomatoes and simmer for a further 5 minutes.

Carefully add this sauce to your roasting tray containing the lamb shanks and cover with foil. Place in the oven for 2 hours, until the meat just falls off the bone.

CREAMY MASHED POTATOES

The creamier the mashed potatoes the better, in my eyes – adding that butter and whisking your potatoes makes it restaurant standard. And always remember to season, too – don't abandon your sides! Put as much love into your mash as you have put into your main dishes. Trust me, it makes all the difference.

SERVES 4 AS A SIDE

5 large floury potatoes (about 1.5 kg/3 lb 5 oz), peeled and cut into eighths

70 g (2½ oz) salted butter

100 ml (3½ fl oz) semi-skimmed milk

salt

Bring a large pan of water to the boil and season with a generous pinch of salt.

Add your potatoes and cook over a medium-high heat for 20 minutes, or until the point of a knife pierces them easily.

Strain your potatoes into a sieve, then return them to the empty saucepan and add your butter and milk.

Mash for 4–5 minutes, until all the lumps have disappeared.

PARMESAN RISOTTO WITH GARLIC PRAWNS

A creamy risotto loaded with Parmesan and juicy prawns is a great combination. It's so rich in flavour, you don't need much of it on your plate. A glass of white wine complements this meal beautifully.

SERVES 4

750 ml (27 fl oz) gluten-free chicken stock

60 g (2¼ oz) unsalted butter

1 onion, diced

4 garlic cloves, 2 crushed, 2 finely chopped

240 g (8½ oz) carnaroli rice

125 ml (4 fl oz) dry white wine

150 g (5½ oz) Parmesan cheese, grated

4 tablespoons double cream

zest of 2 lemons

juice of ½ lemon

olive oil, for frying

2 bird's eye chillies, deseeded and finely sliced

12 large raw peeled prawns, deveined

sea salt flakes and black pepper

lemon wedges, to serve

Pour your stock into a saucepan, bring to a simmer and keep warm.

Place half your butter in a separate saucepan over a medium heat. When melted, add your onion and cook for 4 minutes, until slightly softened.

Add your crushed garlic and cook for 1 minute.

Stir in your rice and 1 teaspoon salt and cook for about 3 minutes, stirring often, until the grains start to become translucent. It's really important to keep stirring so your rice doesn't stick!

Add your white wine and stir for about 2½ minutes, until the pan is almost dry.

Add a cupful of your warm stock and continue cooking and stirring until most of the liquid is absorbed; this will take about 4 minutes.

Continue adding the stock a cup at a time, allowing each addition to be almost fully absorbed before adding the next. When all the stock has been used, the risotto should be moist but not loose, with al dente grains.

Take the pan off the heat and stir in your Parmesan, cream,

lemon zest and half the lemon juice, 1 teaspoon pepper and your remaining butter. Taste and season with extra salt if you like.

Place 2 tablespoons olive oil in a large pan over a low heat, add your chillies and chopped garlic and leave to infuse for 1–2 minutes.

Add your prawns and cook until they're nice and pink; about 3–4 minutes should do it.

Serve your risotto in shallow bowls and top with the prawns, making sure to leave any excess oil in the pan. Squeeze over the remaining lemon juice and add an extra sprinkle of salt and pepper. Sprinkle the chillies over the prawns and add a wedge of lemon on the side of the bowl with the risotto.

TIP

Any leftover risotto can be used to make my Arancini (*see* page 93).

LOBSTER RAVIOLI IN VODKA SAUCE

Lobster on the menu? Wow, that's posh! Combined with tomato sauce and creamy ricotta, it makes a rich and delicious filling for large ravioli served in a vodka-based sauce. Adding a squeeze of fresh lemon juice makes the flavours explode in your mouth!

SERVES 4

1 raw lobster, about 700 g (1 lb 9 oz oz)

170 g (6 oz) ricotta cheese

40 g (2½ oz) sun-dried tomatoes from a jar

15 g (½ oz) fresh flat-leaf parsley, chopped, plus extra sprigs for garnish

zest and juice of ½ lemon

1 egg, beaten

sea salt flakes and pepper

1 lemon, cut into wedges, to serve

For the pasta dough

145 g (5¼ oz) gluten-free plain flour, plus extra for dusting

1 teaspoons xanthan gum

½ teaspoon salt

3 eggs

First make the pasta dough: place the flour, xanthan gum and salt in a bowl and whisk together.

Make a large well in the floured centre and crack in your eggs.

Using a fork, beat the eggs until combined, then gradually incorporate the flour until a dough forms. Shape it into a ball using your hands.

Turn the dough onto a lightly floured work surface and knead until smooth. This usually takes about 2–3 minutes.

Cut the dough into quarters and wrap each piece in clingfilm. Set aside to rest while you begin the lobster filling.

Bring a large pan of water to the boil. Add your lobster and cook for 7–8 minutes. I always set a timer for this, as overcooked lobster is not good!

Meanwhile, place your ricotta and sun-dried tomatoes in a food processor or blender and blitz until smooth and creamy.

Add the chopped parsley, lemon zest and juice and blitz for about 1 minute. Transfer the mixture to a bowl, season well with salt and pepper and set aside.

For the sauce

2 tablespoons olive oil

2 garlic cloves, finely chopped

1 shallot, finely chopped

250 g (9 oz) tomato passata

80 ml (2¾ fl oz) vodka

20 g (¾ oz) fresh flat-leaf parsley, chopped

80 ml (2¾ fl oz) double cream

Once your lobster is done, remove it from the pan and set aside until cool. If you want to speed things up, you can place it in a bowl of iced water.

Using a sharp knife, cut the cooled lobster in half straight down the middle. You'll need to use your muscles to break through the shell, so be careful! Scoop out the white meat and set aside.

Twist off the lobster claws at the knuckle joint.

Holding the large part of a claw on a board with one hand, use the other hand to give it a firm blow with the blunt side of a large knife. This should crack the shell, allowing you to remove the meat in one whole piece for garnish. Repeat this step with each claw.

Finely chop the reserved white meat, add to the ricotta mixture and set aside.

Lightly flour a work surface and roll each piece of pasta dough into a long rectangle about 5 mm (¼ in) thick.

If you have a pasta machine, set it to the widest setting and pass each sheet of rolled-out dough through it twice. Repeat this step, reducing the setting each time, until the dough is 3 mm (⅛ in) thick – you should be able to see your hand through it. This rolling process can also be done by hand. Whichever method you use, be gentle!

Lay a pasta sheet on a lightly floured surface and cut in half widthways. We're now going to make 3 raviolis, so place 3 portions (about a tablespoon each) of your lobster filling on the pasta dough, spaced 5 cm (2 in) apart. Brush beaten egg all over the filling and the dough surrounding it. Cover with the remaining half sheet and press gently around the filling to seal. Using a 10cm (4 in) round cutter, cut out each ravioli.

Repeat the rolling, filling and cutting process with the remaining pieces of dough.

Bring a large pan of water to the boil and season with salt. Lower the heat to medium, add 2 ravioli and cook for about 4 minutes. (Be gentle and don't overcrowd your pan, as you don't want your ravioli to split!)

To make the sauce, place the oil in a large frying pan over a medium heat. When hot, add your garlic and shallot and cook gently, until softened but not brown.

Add the passata and simmer for 4 minutes, then stir in your vodka and simmer for about 7 minutes, until the alcohol has burnt off.

Add a big pinch of salt and a generous amount of black pepper, then stir in the parsley and cream and leave to simmer for a further 2 minutes.

Stir 2 tablespoons of the pasta water into your sauce, then add your ravioli and spoon the sauce over them.

Spoon some sauce into the bottom of each serving bowl, add 3 ravioli and top with some of the reserved lobster claw meat. Garnish with a parsley sprig and a lemon wedge.

Squeeze a little lemon juice over each dish and add a final crack of black pepper before serving.

HEAVEN O'CLOCK

SCHOOL CAKE

FOUR TIERS OF
HEAVEN CAKE

RAINBOW CUPCAKES

SALTED CARAMEL
CHOCOLATE FONDANTS

CARAMEL SHARDS

JAM & COCONUT CAKE

LEMON DRIZZLE CAKE

APPLE CRUMBLE

VANILLA CUSTARD

CHANTILLE WITH
RASPBERRY COULIS

LEMON TART

VANILLA QUENELLES

CHOCOLATE TWISTS

CHOCOLATE
& STRAWBERRY
DREAM PANCAKES

CHOCOLATE
BROWNIES

WHITE CHOCOLATE
& STRAWBERRY
CHEESECAKE

WHITE CHOCOLATE
CHUNK COOKIES

COFFEE & WALNUT
CAKE

CHOCOLATE
STRAWBERRIES

HEAVEN
O'CLOCK

OK, so we're finally here. Are you ready to dive into heaven? No, I'm being serious. These GF desserts are so mouth-watering and good. And I have my sister Milly to thank for that. She opened my eyes to baking, which I used to hate, and her cakes are so much better than what you buy in the shops.

I'm going to be straight up here: I'm tired of trying rubbish GF desserts, tired of sitting in restaurants and only being offered a fruit bowl. I want to dip my spoon into a melting chocolate fondant, or eat piping hot apple crumble, *topping and all*! We should all be able to enjoy sweet food, and we can. I have a wide range of desserts in this chapter, and some fantastic cakes. My famous School Cake recipe (*see* page 152) is so easy and so tasty! I love making food that takes me back to being a kid. Wow, I don't know why I'm speaking as if I'm an oldie here, but it's true – I love going down memory lane. My grandparents used to grow blackberries and apples, and we would pick them, wash them and eat them in our desserts. I want to create that for my children one day too.

The recipes in this chapter are a mixture of 'dinner party' desserts and 'complete pig out at home with your onesie on' desserts. Oh yeah, and before I forget, the chocolate-covered pancakes with strawberries on top are in here too. I have never received so many messages as about that dish! I love that you guys love my cooking. So now you can experiment too. Here we go...

SCHOOL CAKE

I'm always being asked to make this for my friends – everyone loves it! The soft vanilla sponge topped with old-fashioned icing and sprinkles is a little bit of nostalgia, and goes so well with custard. I always eat it warm from the oven. You can't beat it!

MAKES 12 SQUARES ——————————————

225 g (8 oz) unsalted butter, at room temperature

225 g (8 oz) caster sugar

4 eggs

225 g (8 oz) gluten-free self-raising flour

500 g (1 lb 2 oz) icing sugar

4 teaspoons water

coloured sprinkles, for decoration

Preheat your oven to 180°C/160° Fan (350°F), Gas Mark 4. Line the bottom and sides of a 32 x 22 cm (12½ x 8¾ in) traybake tin with non-stick baking paper.

Place your butter and caster sugar in a bowl and beat together until pale and creamy. I use an electric whisk for this.

Beat in your eggs one at a time, making sure each one is incorporated before adding the next.

Sift in your flour and stir until well combined.

Pour your batter into the prepared tin and bake for 50 minutes, or until a metal skewer inserted in the centre of the cake comes out clean. Turn the cake onto a wire rack to cool.

Meanwhile, place your icing sugar in a large bowl and add the measured water in tiny splashes, mixing well between each one. You need to add just enough to make a paste that coats the back of a spoon.

Once your cake has completely cooled, pour your icing on top. Then scatter your colourful sprinkles over the surface and eat straight away!

FOUR TIERS OF HEAVEN CAKE

Have you ever wanted a huge GF birthday cake? Here you go! This layered cake, filled with buttercream and decorated with fancy piping, is lovely and soft, but so high – it's just what you want on your special day! In fact, it's what we all need in our lives! Looks so cute for Insta pics too!

SERVES 12–16

450 g (1 lb) unsalted butter, at room temperature, plus extra for greasing

450 g (1 lb) caster sugar

8 eggs

1 tablespoon vanilla extract

450 g (1 lb) gluten-free self-raising flour

food colouring of your choice (I used pink)

1 x 300 g (10½ oz) jar strawberry jam

glacé cherries, to decorate (optional)

For the buttercream

500g (1 lb 2 oz) unsalted butter, at room temperature

1.5 kg (3 lb 6 oz) icing sugar

3 tablespoons milk

2 tablespoons vanilla extract

Preheat your oven to 180°C/160° Fan (350°F), Gas Mark 4. Butter 4 round shallow loose-bottomed cake tins (20 cm/8 in wide) and line with non-stick baking paper. If you don't have 4 tins, you can make the cakes in batches.

Place your butter and caster sugar in a large bowl and beat until pale and creamy. Beat in your eggs one at a time, then add your vanilla extract. Sift in your flour and beat well to combine.

Pour half the batter into a separate bowl and add your food colouring to it a drop at a time, stirring until you achieve the colour you want. Divide it equally between 2 of the prepared tins and smooth with a knife.

Divide the bowl of plain batter equally between the remaining 2 tins and smooth them too.

Put all 4 of your cake tins into the oven for 30–35 minutes, until a metal skewer inserted into the centre of each cake comes out clean. Leave the cakes to cool in their tins on a wire rack. When cold, turn them out.

Now make the buttercream. Place your butter in a large bowl with about half the icing sugar, the milk and vanilla extract and whisk well. Gradually whisk in the remaining icing sugar until the mixture is light and fluffy.

Place half your buttercream in a separate bowl and use a cocktail stick to add your food colouring to it a drop at a time, stirring until you achieve the colour you want. The other bowl of buttercream is left plain.

Once your cakes are cooled, it's time for the fun part. Place one of your cakes on a stand or plate and spread some of your plain buttercream evenly over the surface. Cover this with a generous layer of jam. Repeat this process until all your tiers are stacked, and don't worry about it being messy.

Use the remaining plain buttercream to cover the top and the sides of your tiered cake.

Grab a silicone piping bag fitted with a star-shaped nozzle and fill it with your coloured buttercream. Now go wild and decorate your cake however you like!

RAINBOW CUPCAKES

Cupcakes never go out of fashion, and this GF recipe is the best! I'm really pleased to have found the perfect ingredients to make them light and fluffy, and they are finished with a thick buttercream. So yummy, I could eat the whole batch!

MAKES 12

200 g (7 oz) unsalted butter, at room temperature

200 g (7 oz) golden caster sugar

3 eggs

2 teaspoons vanilla extract

200 g (7 oz) gluten-free self-raising flour

sprinkles, rainbows or edible glitter, to decorate

For the buttercream

170 g (6 oz) unsalted butter, at room temperature

320 g (11 oz) icing sugar

1 teaspoon vanilla extract

1 tablespoon milk

Preheat your oven to 180°C/160° Fan (350°F), Gas Mark 4. Line a 12-hole cupcake tray with paper cases.

Place your butter and caster sugar in a large bowl and whisk together until pale and creamy.

Add your eggs and vanilla extract and whisk until combined.

Now use a spoon to fold in your flour. When fully incorporated, whisk for a good 3–4 minutes, until light and fluffy.

Spoon the batter into the paper cases, filling them just over halfway.

Bake for 25–30 minutes, until golden, or a metal skewer inserted in the centre comes out clean. Transfer to a wire rack to cool.

Meanwhile, you can make your buttercream. Place your butter and half the icing sugar in a large bowl and whisk until light and creamy. Whisk in the remaining icing sugar a bit at a time, then add your vanilla extract and milk and whisk once more.

When the cupcakes are completely cold, spoon a good tablespoon of buttercream on top of each one and decorate with sprinkles, rainbows or glitter. Be messy – the more rustic the better!

SALTED CARAMEL CHOCOLATE FONDANTS

This is defo the best chocolate dessert. Dark chocolate with a gooey salted caramel middle? Wow, that's literally heaven to me. I make these for special occasions, and they go down a treat!

MAKES 6

100 g (3½ oz) unsalted butter, plus a little melted butter for brushing

dark cocoa powder, for dusting

160 g (5¾ oz) dark chocolate

2 eggs, plus 2 egg yolks

55 g (2 oz) caster sugar

½ teaspoon vanilla extract

100 g (3½ oz) gluten-free plain flour

6 sheets edible gold leaf (optional)

For the salted caramel

125 g (4½ oz) granulated white sugar

35 ml (1¼ fl oz) water

100 ml (3½ fl oz) double cream

30 g (1 oz) unsalted butter

½ teaspoon vanilla extract

½ teaspoon salt

Start by making your salted caramel. Place your sugar and water in a saucepan over a low heat and stir continuously until the sugar has dissolved. The liquid will look a little cloudy, but there should be no sugar granules left.

Turn the heat up to medium so that the mixture starts to bubble, then turn the heat up higher and STOP stirring. Don't touch it anymore, but keep an eye on it as it becomes amber-coloured. This should take 8–10 minutes.

Take the pan off the heat and pour your cream in carefully, as the mixture will bubble vigorously. Now whisk until combined. It will feel tough to do this, but don't stop until you have a smooth caramel.

Add your butter and whisk until completely melted. Now whisk in your vanilla, and finally your salt.

Pour the salted caramel into ice-cube trays and place in the freezer until almost fully frozen.

Meanwhile, preheat your oven to 180°C/160°C Fan (350°F), Gas Mark 4. Brush 6 ramekins (about 8 x 4 cm /3 x ¾ in) with your extra melted butter, line with non-stick baking paper, then lightly brush the paper with more butter. Lightly dust the buttered paper with cocoa powder.

Sit a heatproof bowl over a pan of simmering water, making sure the water isn't actually touching the bowl. Now place your measured butter and chocolate in the bowl and allow to melt. Once melted, stir together and set aside.

Place your eggs, egg yolks, sugar and vanilla extract in a clean bowl and whisk until pale, fluffy and doubled in size.

Whisk in the melted chocolate, then sift in your flour and fold it in with a spoon or spatula.

Spoon this fondant mixture into your prepared ramekins until about half full.

Depending on their size, place 1 or 2 of your caramel ice cubes in the middle of each ramekin. Spoon in a bit more fondant, covering the ice cubes and keeping them about 1cm (½ in) below the rim.

Place your ramekins in a baking tray and bake for 20 minutes. Your fondants will rise just above the rim of the dishes, but if they look wobbly, give them another 5 minutes. Allow to rest for 1 minute, before turning upside down onto serving plates. Peel off the paper. Brush on the gold leaf, if using, and dust with more cocoa powder.

Make sure to serve these straight away, while they're gorgeously hot and gooey inside. If you want to be really fancy, you can garnish them with my Caramel Shards (*see* page 164).

CARAMEL SHARDS

Beautiful caramel shards are surprisingly easy to make, and add a touch of sophistication to any dessert!

SERVES 6 ───────────────────────────

50 g (1¾ oz) caster sugar

50 ml (2 fl oz) water

1 tablespoon liquid glucose

Start by covering a large board or plate with non-stick baking paper, and filling the sink with iced water.

Place your sugar in a heavy-based saucepan over a medium heat and add your measured water and liquid glucose. Stir together until the sugar dissolves and the mixture becomes less cloudy.

Leave to simmer and bubble until it turns a golden colour, about 1–2 minutes. Keep an eye on it!

Take the pan off the heat and dip the base into the iced water for just a few seconds. If left for any longer, the caramel stiffens and becomes unworkable.

Dip a fork into the soft caramel and flick it back and forth in every direction across your lined board to create whatever shapes you like.

Set aside to cool and firm up, then break into pieces and store in an airtight container.

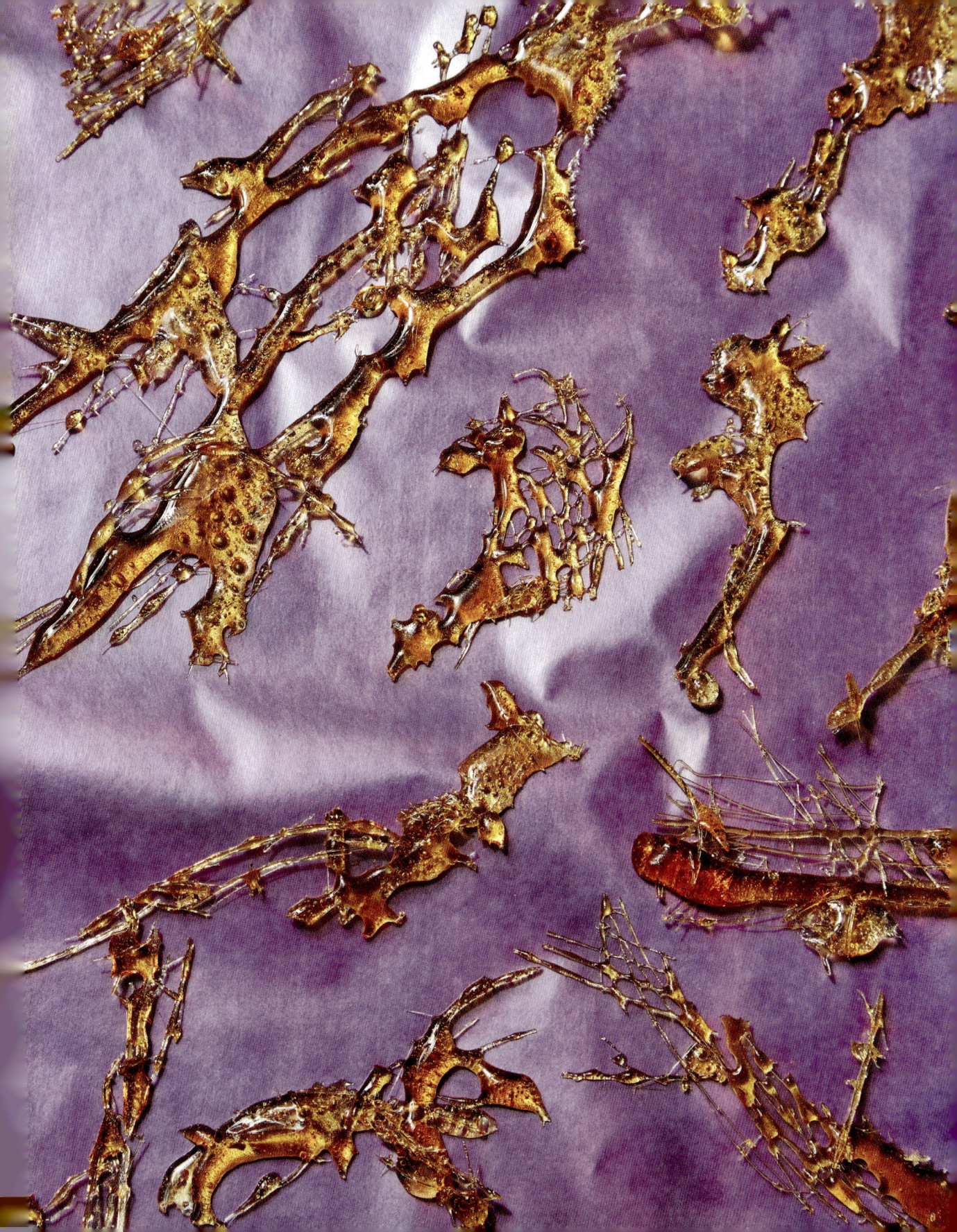

JAM & COCONUT CAKE

Another school classic. There's something really comforting about jam on a cake. Here its tangy flavour goes so well with the coconut sprinkles. I like to serve it warm with custard.

MAKES 12 SLICES ——————————————————————

225 g (8 oz) unsalted butter, at room temperature

225 g (8 oz) caster sugar

4 eggs

225 g (8 oz) gluten-free self-raising flour

For the decoration

1 x 300 g (10½ oz) jar strawberry jam

100 g (3½ oz) desiccated coconut

Preheat your oven to 180°C/160° Fan (350°F), Gas Mark 4. Set out a 32 x 22 cm (12½ x 8¾ in) traybake tin. Line the bottom and sides with non-stick baking paper.

Place your butter and sugar in a large bowl and whisk together until pale and creamy.

Beat in your eggs one at a time, making sure each one is incorporated before adding the next.

Sift in your flour and stir well to combine.

Pour your batter into the prepared tin and bake for 50 minutes, or until a metal skewer inserted in the centre of the cake comes out clean.

Turn the cake onto a wire rack and leave to cool.

Once cooled, peel off the paper, turn the cake over and spread a thick layer of jam across the top. Sprinkle over the coconut and serve!

LEMON DRIZZLE CAKE

A lemon drizzle cake, so sweet and soft, is way up there on my list of favourites! Eating it fresh from the oven is amazing, so good that I could eat it for dinner. I strongly advise you to try this one!

MAKES 12 SLICES

225 g (8 oz) unsalted butter, at room temperature

225 g (8 oz) caster sugar

4 eggs

225 g (8 oz) gluten-free self-raising flour

zest of 4 lemons

lemon slices, to decorate (optional)

For the drizzle

juice of 4 lemons

170 g (6 oz) caster sugar

Preheat your oven to 180°C/160° Fan (350°F), Gas Mark 4. Line a loose-bottomed 22 cm (8 in) square cake tin with non-stick baking paper.

Place your butter and caster sugar in a large bowl and beat together until pale and creamy.

Add your eggs one at a time, beating well between each addition.

Sift in your flour, add your lemon zest and fold in until well combined.

Spoon the batter into your prepared tin and level the surface.

Bake for 45–50 minutes, until a metal skewer inserted in the centre comes out clean. Set aside, still in the tin, while you make your lemon drizzle.

Place the lemon juice and caster sugar in a bowl and mix well.

Prick the warm cake with a skewer or fork, then pour the drizzle over it. The syrup will sink in, while the sugar will form a lovely crisp topping.

Leave the cake in the tin to cool completely, then carefully transfer it to a plate and serve. I like to add a few lemon slices for decoration.

APPLE CRUMBLE

Classic crumble has been my family's go-to dessert for generations, especially after a Sunday roast. We always make it with a thick GF topping, which everyone loves, and I wouldn't mind betting it becomes your favourite dessert too. Serve it with cream or my Vanilla Custard (*see* page 172)!

SERVES 4

4 Bramley apples, peeled, cored and cut into even-sized chunks

4 tablespoons caster sugar

½ lemon

For the crumble

175 g (6 oz) gluten-free plain flour

140 g (5 oz) caster sugar, plus extra for sprinkling

pinch of salt

140 g (5 oz) cold butter, diced

100 g (3½ oz) gluten-free oats

Preheat your oven to 180°C/160° Fan (350°F), Gas Mark 4. Set out a 20 cm (8 in) round baking dish.

Place your apples and 2 tablespoons of the sugar in a saucepan and add enough water to cover them. Bring to the boil and cook until the apples are just soft enough to pierce with a knife, but still holding their shape.

In the meantime, start your crumble topping. Place your flour, sugar and salt in a large bowl. Add your butter and rub it in with your fingertips until the mixture resembles breadcrumbs.

Now mix in in your oats. Shake the bowl so that any large pieces come to the surface, then break these up into smaller bits.

Strain your apples, being careful not to break the chunks, and put them into your baking dish.

Sprinkle the remaining 2 tablespoons sugar over the apples and add a squeeze of lemon juice.

Spread your crumble mixture evenly over the apples, then add a final sprinkling of sugar.

Bake for 35–40 minutes, until golden brown, and leave to cool a little before serving.

VANILLA CUSTARD

You can't beat a rich thick custard. It goes with everything – my School Cake and Jam & Coconut Cake (*see* pages 152 and 167), obviously my Apple Crumble (*see* page 170) and anything else you fancy pouring it over. Enjoy!

SERVES 4

500 ml (18 fl oz) double cream

1 vanilla pod, split open lengthways

4 egg yolks

100 g (3½ oz) caster sugar

Place your cream in a large saucepan over a medium heat. Scrape in the vanilla seeds, stir together, then heat until the cream begins to simmer and becomes infused with the vanilla flavour.

Place your egg yolks and caster sugar in a large bowl and whisk until light and creamy.

Transfer your infused cream to a clean saucepan over a medium heat. Slowly pour in the egg mixture, whisking as you do so, and continue whisking for 4–6 minutes, or until the mixture is custard-like and coats the back of a spoon. It's important to do this step gradually and whisk thoroughly or you'll end up with scrambled eggs!

CHANTILLE WITH RASPBERRY COULIS

This is my personal dinner party fave. Light meringue is mixed with whipped cream, then frozen and served with my raspberry coulis. It's quick and easy to put together, but make sure you give yourself enough time to freeze it! You need to prepare this the day before you want to serve it.

SERVES 8–10

500 ml (18 fl oz) double cream

8 meringue nests

1 tablespoon vanilla extract

raspberries, to decorate

For the raspberry coulis

500g (1 lb 2 oz) raspberries

3 heaped tablespoons icing sugar

Pour your cream into a large bowl. Using an electric whisk, beat the cream until it thickens just enough to cling to the beaters.

Break your meringues into bite-sized pieces. Add them, and the vanilla extract, to the whipped cream, and fold together with a large spoon.

Spoon your mixture into into a 22 cm (8½ in) brioche mould lined with clingfilm, and level out the surface.

Place in the freezer overnight.

To make the raspberry coulis, place three-quarters of your raspberries in a saucepan over a medium heat and add your icing sugar. Cook for 5–10 minutes, stirring now and then, until the raspberries have broken down to a pulp.

Using the back of a large spoon, press the fruit mixture through a sieve into a bowl to get rid of the seeds and any lumps. Set aside to cool.

When you're ready to serve your chantille, place the mould upside down onto a serving plate. Lift off the mould and gently pull the clingfilm at the base to remove. Pour over the raspberry coulis and and put the remaining fresh raspberries on top!

LEMON TART

It's so nice to eat GF tarts, isn't it? And this one seems to explode in the mouth with just the right amount of lemon flavour. Not too sharp and not too sweet. Serve with whipped cream or one of my Vanilla Quenelles (*see* page 178) on the side to make it look fancy and you're ready to go!

SERVES 10–12

2 eggs

100 g (3½ oz) caster sugar

zest and juice of 4 lemons

150 ml (5 fl oz) double cream

For the pastry

300 g (10½ oz) gluten-free plain flour, plus extra for dusting

1 teaspoon xanthan gum

3 tablespoons caster sugar

pinch of salt

145 g (5¼ oz) cold unsalted butter, roughly diced, plus extra for greasing

2 egg yolks

1 whole egg, beaten, for brushing

Preheat your oven to 180°C/160° Fan (350°F), Gas Mark 4. Butter a loose-bottomed 22 cm (9 in) tart tin.

Start by making the pastry. Place your flour in a large bowl and mix in the xanthan gum, caster sugar and salt.

Add your butter and rub in using your fingertips until the mixture resembles breadcrumbs.

Mix in your egg yolks until a dough forms, then shape it into a ball. Wrap in clingfilm and freeze for 30 minutes.

Lightly flour a work surface and roll out the chilled dough until it's about 5 mm (¼ in) thick. Use it to line the prepared tin, then trim off the excess and prick the base with a fork. Line the pastry case with a piece of crumpled baking paper and fill with baking beans or rice. Bake for 15 minutes.

Remove the baking beans and paper, and brush the pastry case with your beaten egg. Return it to the oven for another 7 minutes, then set aside to cool.

Meanwhile, make the filling. Place your eggs and caster sugar in a large bowl and whisk together. Add your lemon zest and juice, then mix in your double cream until fully combined.

Pour the filling into your pastry case and bake for 40 minutes. Set the tart aside to cool completely, then refrigerate until firm.

When you're ready to serve it, carefully transfer the tart to a serving plate. If you have a blowtorch, you can lightly brown the surface if you wish.

VANILLA QUENELLES

I've always preferred a spoonful of whipped cream to ice cream as an accompaniment. Adding a quenelle to your dessert doesn't only look impressive, it also gives you that freshness you may want with a gooey chocolate brownie or fondant. Once you get the hang of the spoon movements to shape the quenelles, you'll be a pro in no time – impress your guests!

SERVES 10–12, AS AN ACCOMPANIMENT ————————————————————

300 ml (10 fl oz) double cream

2 tablespoons vanilla extract

Pour your cream into a large bowl. Using an electric whisk, beat the cream until it thickens just enough to cling to the beaters.

Stir in your vanilla extract.

Get 2 tablespoons and dip them into a bowl of hot water. Use one of them to scoop up a mound of cream. Transfer it to the other hot spoon, then pass it back and forth between the spoons until you have formed a three-sided oval.

Transfer to a large plate and continue making quenelles in the same way, dipping the spoons in hot water each time, until all the cream has been used. Place in the fridge until required.

CHOCOLATE TWISTS

These little treats are so easy to make and so yummy! Twists of pastry and chocolate cooked together just have to work, don't they? A cute tray of goodness to serve your friends!

SERVES 4

1 x 280 g (10 oz) packet ready-rolled gluten-free puff pastry

250 g (9 oz) chocolate and hazelnut spread

1 egg, beaten

1 tablespoon sugar (optional)

Preheat your oven to 190°C/170° Fan (375°F), Gas Mark 5 and line a baking sheet with non-stick baking paper.

Unroll your pastry on a work surface and cut the sheet in half widthwise.

Smooth half your chocolate spread over your first piece of pastry, leaving a 1 cm (½ in) clear border around all the edges.

With one of the longest sides closest to you, roll the pastry into a long, thin log.

Cut the log in half lengthways from end to end, so you're left with two halves, with the centres facing up. Pinch the top ends together and carefully overlap the 2 pieces together to form a twist. Pinch the ends together to hold the twist in place.

Repeat the filling, rolling and twisting process with the second piece of puff pastry.

Place the twists on the prepared baking sheet and brush them with the beaten egg. Sprinkle with the extra sugar if you wish, then bake for 25–30 minutes, until golden brown.

Transfer to a wire rack and leave to cool for at least 10 minutes before slicing and serving.

CHOCOLATE & STRAWBERRY DREAM PANCAKES

As you may already know, I love pancakes! My GF stacking pancakes have gone down so well on my social media that I have to include the recipes here! Don't forget to add your toppings! This is the ultimate pig-out dessert and I love it!

MAKES 12

450 g (1 lb) gluten-free self-raising flour

2 eggs

300 ml (10 fl oz) semi-skimmed milk

olive oil, for frying

chocolate and hazelnut spread

5 strawberries, quartered or halved

2 tablespoons icing sugar

Place your flour, eggs and milk in a large bowl and whisk until smooth.

Put 1 tablespoon olive oil in a large non-stick frying pan over a low heat. When hot, add 1 heaped tablespoon of your pancake batter and swirl it around until you have a small circle about 5 mm (¼ in) thick. Depending on the size of the pan, add another 1 or 2 spoonfuls in the same way. The circles look thin, but they will rise, don't you worry!

Turn the heat up to medium and cook for about 1½ minutes on each side, until fluffed up and lightly speckled brown. You'll know when they're ready.

Transfer the pancakes to a plate and keep warm while you make as many more pancakes as you can with the remaining batter. Remember to heat a spoonful of oil for each batch.

Serve the pancakes in stacks of 3, spreading 2 tablespoons chocolate spread between each layer and scattering the strawberries on top.

Finish with a dusting of icing sugar and enjoy!

CHOCOLATE BROWNIES

Who doesn't love a batch of freshly cooked brownies to dip into? I always do, and it's become a joke how amazing these taste. Heat them up and serve with a scoop of ice cream. Wow, insane!

MAKES 12

170 g (6 oz) unsalted butter, at room temperature

200 g (7 oz) caster sugar

90 g (3¼ oz) brown sugar

3 large eggs

1 teaspoon vanilla extract

3 tablespoons chocolate and hazelnut spread

70 g (2½ oz) gluten-free self-raising flour

40 g (1½ oz) cocoa powder

100 g (3½ oz) white chocolate, broken into small pieces

Preheat your oven to 200°C/180° Fan (400°F), Gas Mark 6. Line the bottom and sides of a deep 30 x 20 cm (12 x 8 in) baking tray with non-stick baking paper.

Place your butter in a large bowl, add your 2 sugars and whisk together until smooth and creamy.

Add your eggs one at a time, beating well between each addition.

Now whisk in your vanilla extract and chocolate and hazelnut spread.

Sift in your flour and cocoa powder, then fold in with a spoon until completely combined.

Finally, fold in your white chocolate pieces.

Pour your brownie mixture into the prepared tray and smooth the surface.

Bake for 50 minutes, reducing the heat to 180°C/160°C Fan (350°F), Gas Mark 4 after 20 minutes.

Set aside to cool before cutting into pieces and serving.

WHITE CHOCOLATE & STRAWBERRY CHEESECAKE

Believe me when I tell you that this is the best cheesecake you will ever eat. I have to give credit to my sister Milly, who has smashed this recipe for years! White chocolate and strawberries are an irresistible combo, so try it and thank me later! You'll need to start making this the day before you want to serve it, as the cheesecake needs to set in the fridge overnight, but it's worth the wait.

SERVES 12

150 g (5½ oz) unsalted butter, melted, plus extra for greasing

100 g (3½ oz) gluten-free digestive biscuits, crushed into crumbs

400 g (14 oz) white chocolate

500 g (1 lb 2 oz) cream cheese

300 ml (10 fl oz) double cream

300 g (10½ oz) icing sugar

For the strawberry compote

600 g (1 lb 5 oz) fresh strawberries

75 g (2¾ oz) white caster sugar

2 tablespoons fresh lemon juice

6g (½ sachet) gelatine

Generously grease the bottom and sides of a 20 cm (8 in) springform cake tin with the extra butter.

Place your crushed biscuits in a bowl, add your melted butter and mix well until the mixture has the consistency of damp sand.

Tip your biscuit mixture into the prepared tin, spread it out evenly, then use the bottom of a glass to press it down firmly.

Sit a heatproof bowl over a pan of simmering water, making sure the water isn't actually touching the bowl. Place your chocolate in the prepared bowl and leave to melt. Set aside to cool slightly.

Meanwhile, place your cream cheese and double cream in a clean bowl and beat until the mixture has thickened.

Stir in your melted chocolate, then sift in your icing sugar and fold together with a spoon, ensuring there are no lumps.

Pour the mixture onto the biscuit base and smooth out the top using a spoon. Place in the refrigerator to set overnight.

When you are ready to make your compote, place 500g (1 lb 2 oz) of your strawberries in a saucepan over a low heat. Add your sugar and lemon juice, stir together and bring to a simmer. Allow to continue simmering for 5 minutes until the sugar has dissolved and the fruit is soft.

Using a hand blender, blitz the mixture until it's smooth. Stir in your powdered gelatine and leave to cool to room temperature.

Pour the cooled compote on top of your cheesecake and refrigerate until the jelly has set.

To serve, carefully remove the cake from the springform tin. I like to halve the remaining strawberries and use them to decorate my cheesecake.

WHITE CHOCOLATE CHUNK COOKIES

These are sooooo soft!

MAKES 12

150 g (5½ oz) unsalted butter, melted

200 g (7 oz) caster sugar

1 large egg

300 g (10½ oz) gluten-free self-raising flour

1 tablespoon baking powder

225 g (8 oz) white chocolate, broken into small chunks

Place the melted butter in a large bowl, add the caster sugar and whisk until combined.

Add the egg and whisk again until you have a runny batter.

Place the flour and baking powder in a separate bowl, then pour in the batter and fold together using a large spoon. Keep mixing to make sure there are no lumps!

Stir in three-quarters of your chocolate, then use your hands to form the mixture into a thick, sticky dough.

Wrap the dough in clingfilm and refrigerate for as long as you can, certainly no less than 6 hours. The cooler your dough, the less likely your cookies are to spread into each other while baking.

When you are ready to bake, preheat your oven to 180°C/160°C Fan (350°F), Gas Mark 4. Line a baking sheet with non-stick baking paper.

Divide your chilled dough into 12 equal pieces (about 2 tablespoons each) and roll into balls. Place them on the prepared baking sheet, leaving a good gap between them, then flatten with the palm of your hand.

Press a few of the remaining white chocolate chunks on top of each cookie.

Bake for 13 minutes, then remove from the oven – the cookies will look very soft and underbaked. Leave them on the baking tray for 20 minutes to cool down and firm up, then transfer to a wire rack to cool completely.

The best way to enjoy these is heated up. Give them 5 minutes in a medium-hot oven, or pop a cookie or two in the microwave for 20 seconds. Yum!

COFFEE & WALNUT CAKE

We're all fans of this classic cake in my house, especially that buttercream topping! Fresh sponge cake with a hint of coffee beans and a walnut crunch really turns this into an afternoon tea special, but I like to think it's the ideal slice with a cuppa at any time of day. I love having a selection of GF cakes in this book, as us GF peeps rarely get options when we're out. Here, you're spoilt for choice.

SERVES 8–10

225 g (8 oz) unsalted butter, at room temperature, plus extra for greasing

225 g (8 oz) caster sugar

4 large eggs

2 heaped teaspoons coffee granules dissolved in 50 ml (2 fl oz) hot water

225 g (8 oz) gluten-free self-raising flour

100 g (3½ oz) walnuts, chopped

handful walnut halves, to decorate

For the buttercream

125 g (4½ oz) unsalted butter, at room temperature

225 g (8 oz) icing sugar

3 teaspoons coffee granules dissolved in 1 teaspoon water

Preheat your oven to 190°C/170° Fan (375°F), Gas Mark 5. Set out a lined 900 g (2 lb) loaf tin.

Place your butter and sugar in a large bowl and whisk together until pale and creamy.

Beat in your eggs one at a time, making sure each one is incorporated before adding the next.

Add your dissolved coffee and mix well.

Using a wooden spoon, fold in your flour and chopped walnuts until fully combined.

Pour your batter into the prepared tin and bake for 40 minutes, or until a metal skewer inserted in the centre of the cake comes out clean.

Turn the cake onto a wire rack and leave to cool.

Meanwhile, make your buttercream. Place your butter and icing sugar in a small bowl and beat together until nice and smooth.

Add your dissolved coffee and mix well.

Once your cake has cooled completely, spread the buttercream over the top. Decorate with the walnut halves and enjoy!

CHOCOLATE STRAWBERRIES

Girls or guys night in? Need something to feed the group? Don't worry, this is so easy and looks so cute that everyone will be impressed. So get your chocolate out and start melting! The more the better, I say!

MAKES 15–20

3 x 100 g (3½ oz) bars of white chocolate, broken into pieces

pink food colouring

500 g (1 lb 2 oz) strawberries, stems left in place for ease of dipping

Sit a heatproof bowl over a pan of simmering water, making sure the water isn't actually touching the bowl.

Place your chocolate in the prepared bowl and leave to melt.

Once the chocolate has melted, put one-third of it in a separate bowl and set aside – you'll need this later, for your white chocolate drizzle. Add a few drops of food colouring to the remaining chocolate and stir until it's a nice even colour. You can add more if you want a deeper shade of pink.

Set out a large tray. Dip the strawberries into the melted pink chocolate one at a time and place them on your tray.

Using a spoon, drizzle the white chocolate over the dipped strawberries. This will create a gorgeous 2-layer effect.

Leave to set in the refrigerator for a few hours before serving.

So, that's it guys – I've let you into my kitchen, told you a few stories and hopefully taught you a thing or two about making things gluten-free. Mission complete!

Honestly, thank you to every person who has followed my journey so far, and for every message I have received about my food. I appreciate it all. Now go and spread the word to the people who need educating that all of us with gluten and wheat allergies want to eat normal food too! Haha!

Love you all,

Megan x

UK/US GLOSSARY

UK	US
baking paper	baking parchment
baking sheet	cookie sheet
baking tray	baking sheet
cake tin	cake pan
caster sugar	superfine sugar
chickpeas	garbanzo beans
chilli flakes	red pepper flakes
clingilm	plastic wrap
coriander, fresh	cilantro
cornflour	cornstarch
courgette	zucchini
dark chocolate	bittersweet chocolate
double cream	heavy cream
egg, medium (UK)	egg, large (US)
frying pan	skillet
gherkin	pickle
glacé cherries	candied cherries
grill	broiler
icing sugar	confectioner's sugar
kitchen paper	paper towels
lengthways	lengthwise
passata	strained/sieved tomatoes
pepper	bell pepper
plain flour	all-purpose flour
prawns	shrimp
rapeseed oil	canola oil
rocket	arugula
self-raising flour	self-rising flour
starter	appetizer
tomato puree	tomato paste

INDEX

ACKNOWLEDGEMENTS

Thank you to everyone who helped make this book happen.

Eleanor Maxfield, thank you for commissioning this book, for being so hands-on, so lovely and ensuring the whole book looks and reads the way it does!

Jaz Bahra, thank you for bringing my visions to life and for making me laugh so hard on shoot days.

Alex Stetter, thank you for checking everything to make sure my recipes are perfect, I really appreciate it.

Charlotte Sanders and Hazel O'Brien, thank you for making sure this book is going to be seen by everybody who needs it, thank you for creating a great campaign for this book.

George Brooker, appreciate you working around my crazy schedule!

Lisa Pinnell, your production skills are wonderful.

Louise Hagger, your photos are unreal and I couldn't be happier with how amazing the food looks.

Sophie Bronze, thank you for your work understanding my perfectionist ways.

Alexander Breeze, you had so many cute options for me to choose from and helped set the scene for each image perfectly.

Becks Wilkinson, a true wizard in the kitchen and your work is so appreciated, thanks for your patience, we got there in the end.

Samantha McWilliam – Thank you to my amazing make-up artist for your magic.

Jade Reuben, my manager, thank you for making this dream become a reality, seven years in the making and for being the inspo behind the chocolate strawberries.

Bold Management – Jade, Kate, Martin, Jackie, Joe, Felan and Lauren, thank you for being the best management team.

Jo Bell, my wonderful book agent, thank you for always believing in me and keeping us all so organized.

To my Mum, thank you for bringing me up in a loving household, always full of good home-cooked food and teaching me how to cook gluten-free from scratch.

Milly, thank you for all your amazing cooking tips and late-night FaceTimes. If it wasn't for you, I wouldn't know how to bake a thing.

Nan – Thank you for being the best critic in the world.

Don't EVER apologize for being gluten-free – from your GF queen

ABOUT MEGAN

Singer-songwriter Megan McKenna first came to prominence as a reality television personality. In 2017, she travelled to Nashville to experience the country music scene that she'd always loved for her ITV series *There's Something About Megan*. The show's success resulted in her debut country album *Story of Me* being released in 2018, with two singles hitting number one and two on British iTunes, knocking Taylor Swift and Pink off the top of the chart. The following year, Megan won *The X Factor: Celebrity*, with her performances firing her into the iTunes Top 5 during every week of the competition.

Megan continues to write and record original music, often visiting LA and Nashville, where she has written songs with huge hitmakers including Toby Gad (John Legend, Beyoncé), Mozella (Miley Cyrus, Ellie Goulding, Kelly Clarkson) and Amy Wadge (Ed Sheeran, Camila Cabello). In 2021, Megan supported Tom Jones on his Summer tour, performed on the main stage at the Isle of Wight festival, headlined her own shows, as well as completing a full UK and Ireland arena tour, supporting and performing alongside Michael Ball and Alfie Boe. Megan also reached the final of BBC's Celebrity MasterChef – and because Megan suffers from coeliac disease, all the dishes she prepared on the show were gluten-free.